MAKING
Mechanical
CARDS

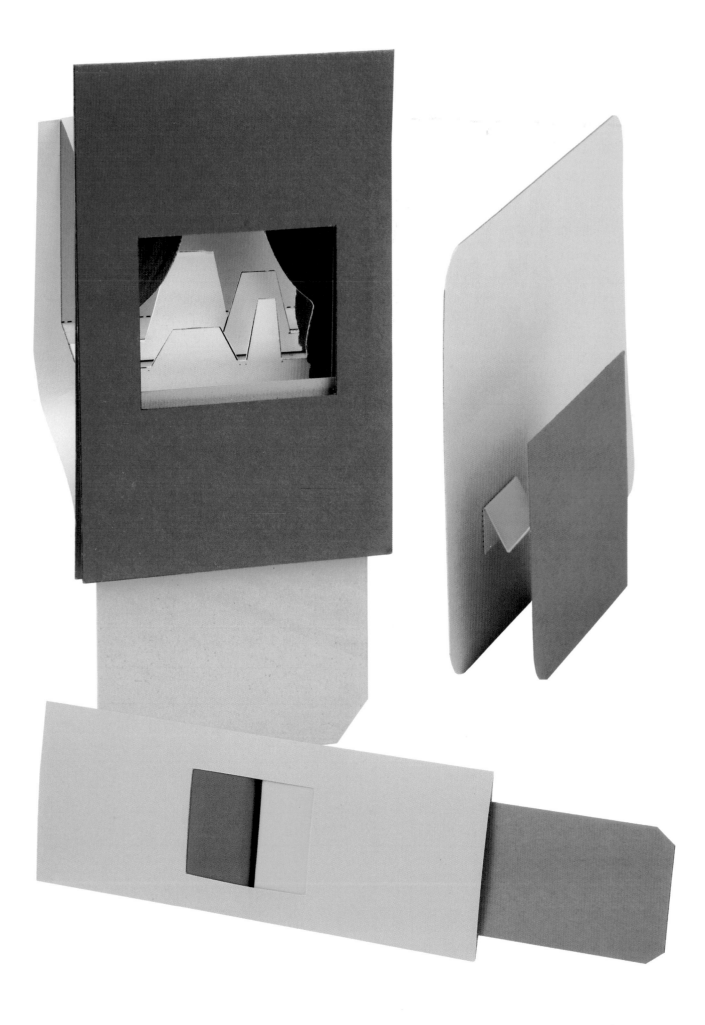

MAKING
Mechanical
CARDS

25 PAPER-ENGINEERED DESIGNS

SHEILA STURROCK

GUILD OF MASTER
CRAFTSMAN PUBLICATIONS LTD

Acknowledgements

I wish to express my gratitude to Philip Wild who, without any
previous knowledge of paper engineering, tested the templates
and instructions for accuracy using only the most basic equipment.

First published 2009 by
Guild of Master Craftsman Publications Ltd
Castle Place, 166 High Street,
Lewes, East Sussex BN7 1XU

Text © Sheila Sturrock, 2009
© in the Work GMC Publications, 2009

ISBN 978-1-86108-635-8

A catalogue record for this book is available from the British Library.

Associate Publisher: Jonathan Bailey
Production Manager: Jim Bulley
Managing Editor: Gerrie Purcell
Senior Project Editor: Dominique Page
Managing Art Editor: Gilda Pacitti
Designer: John Hawkins
Photographer: Anthony Bailey

Set in ITC Kabel and The Sans

Colour origination by GMC Reprographics
Printed and bound in Thailand by Kyodo Nation Printing

CONTENTS

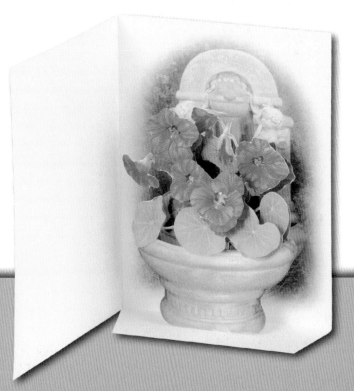

INTRODUCTION

In December 1991 Laura Seddon, a retired teacher and noted collector of glass and ephemera, donated over 31,500 Victorian and Edwardian greetings cards to Manchester Polytechnic (now Manchester Metropolitan University) in the north of England. The cards, collected over a period of 20 years and mounted in 274 volumes, were published in a catalogue which took Mrs. Seddon 5 years to complete and were intended as a source of reference for those interested in Victorian and Edwardian social history.

My son was working in the art and design department when the catalogues were delivered and noted that several of the volumes contained examples of moving and mechanical cards. Aware that paper engineering had been my interest since childhood he made arrangements for me to view the collection. The original visit was to be for one day but this stretched to monthly visits for many years, during which I was given the opportunity to view other collections and ephemera in

the University Special Collection reference section of the library. The British Printer magazines were particularly interesting, giving an insight into printing processes, stationers, card designers and the latest machinery and tools. Ladies' magazines were another source of information, articles appearing annually to coincide with Valentine's Day. In 1995, Mrs. Seddon catalogued and donated her collection of 1,095 Valentine cards to the University and I was given the opportunity to database them. It was entirely through this Manchester contact that I was able to view major card collections in other parts of the country, many of which contained movable cards.

The cards featured in this book are based on Victorian and Edwardian designs, and over the next few pages you'll see some original examples. You'll also discover a little of the history of greetings cards. If you find you're as interested in mechanical cards as I am, I would recommend you visit some of the wonderful collections that open to the public so that you can view the originals for yourself (see page 159 for a list of collections).

Sheila Sturrock

Greetings cards have a rich and interesting history, and their origins can be traced back over several centuries. During the fifteenth century, meditational pictures were painted in monasteries in Catholic Europe, as an offshoot of manuscript illumination. Picture sizes varied from matchbox to postcard with the central illustration generally painted in gouache on vellum or embroidered on paper, silk or linen. Large areas perforated with extremely fine paper cut lace (Spitzenbilder) surrounded the illustrations. Following the invention of the printing press, towards the end of the seventeenth century, Spitzenbilder cards were mass-produced in Augsburg, Munich, Nuremburg and Vienna. They were given to celebrate weddings, confirmations, Holy Communion and funerals, and were undoubtedly the precursor of the English Valentine, early examples of which included hand paper-pricked or paper-cut lace.

Not all cards were sent with good intentions, however. Cards with crude caricatures and spiteful verses were extremely popular in the early nineteenth century, as the recipient paid the postage and would have the dubious pleasure of paying to be insulted.

Valentines

The custom of sending anonymous tokens of affection appears to have evolved from a conflation of various ancient customs that took place at the Roman festival, Lupercalia, February 13th to 15th, where lots were drawn by youths to find partners. February 14th has, therefore, been associated with romance since early on.

Early hand-made Valentines were watercolours, pen-and-ink sketches or novel cards based on word puzzles; for instance, the eternal love knot and the origami-style puzzle purse. The commercial paper Valentines, usually of decorated design with sentimental verses, were hand-coloured wood-cut and copper-engraved designs. These first appeared

in England during the very late eighteenth century. Some had side panels opening to show cupid watching over a sailor or churches with opening doors to reveal a marriage ceremony.

Embossed borders, introduced around 1830, were created by laying the paper on a steel die and beating it with lead hammers. The invention of paper lace is attributed to Joseph Addenbrooke who filed off the raised embossing to produce paper lace from which developed cameo lace. The manufacture of embossed and paper lace provided a background for lithographed Valentines. Specially trained women applied gold and silver embossing to the lace paper or cut paper cages in which an overlay of paper was cut spirally and attached to the centre. When pulled, a hidden message or picture was revealed. Other cards included aerophane (a fine semi-transparent fabric) to give soft background effects, hand-coloured chromo-lithographs with movable centres revealing cherubs and tokens of sentiment, inserts printed on satin, and woven greetings. Three-dimensional cards were created using paper springs and elaborate cards produced with up to four layers of paper lace and decorated with imported German scraps, mother-of-pearl, shells, human hair, feathers, cloth flowers and other embellishments.

Lace Valentine cards reached the height of popularity during the 1850s. Printers set up assembly lines of women and children to glue and attach sentiments to the paper lace. At their height, England exported large numbers of cards to America and the colonies. During the 1850s Australian gold rush, London stationers received urgent messages from gold miners prepared to pay £10 to £20, or one bag of gold, for a Valentine card.

In 1847, Esther Howland, daughter of a Massachusetts stationer in the US, received a paper lace Valentine from England. She began making her own designs for which her brother, a stationery company sales representative, took orders worth over $5,000 during his travels through New England. She purchased embossed and perforated blanks from England, decorative material from New York and set up her card-making business. The business flourished and in 1881 was sold to the Whitney Company who became the largest manufacturer of mass-produced Valentines in America.

By the mid 1860s, public interest in paper lace cards had declined. Alternative designs included shaped and mechanical cards using rotating disks, pull-tab flower cards, opening dimensional scenes, fans, hold-to-light cards, concertina panoramas and transformation scenes. Many mechanical cards were so elaborate that they could almost be classed as mechanical toys.

The first mechanical card was produced in Berlin, revealing a fully rigged ship. Such was the demand for the card that skilled men were sought to construct it. It is believed that the card's fortunate inventor made sufficient money to build a real ship in which he sailed to America.

Christmas Cards

Improvements in transport and communication together with the reform of the postal service by Rowland Hill in 1840 meant that post could be sent quickly, efficiently and inexpensively to all parts of the country, payment being made by the sender. Hill was assisted by Henry Cole, later to become Sir Henry Cole, founder of the Victoria & Albert Museum in London. Cole was particularly interested in the arts, and in 1843 he requested that his friend, John Horsley, design a card he could send to his friends at Christmas. The first Christmas card was a traditional triptych design, the two outer panels depicting acts of charity, feeding the hungry and clothing the poor and in the centre was a family gathering. The first envelope-folding machine was demonstrated by De la Rue at the Great Exhibition, London, in 1851. Envelopes enabled mechanical cards to be sent safely through the post.

The introduction of commercial Christmas cards around 1860 spelled the demise of the Valentine card. Louis Prang, a German immigrant who started a small lithographic business near Boston, Massachusetts, in 1856, is generally credited with the start of the greeting-card industry in America. In the early

1870s, his Christmas cards found a ready market in England and in 1875 he introduced his first complete line of Christmas cards to the American public. Within ten years of founding his firm, he had perfected the colour lithographic process to a point where his reproductions of great paintings surpassed those of other graphic arts craftsmen in both America and Great Britain. Prang's cards reached their height of popularity in the early 1890s but when cheap imitative imports began to flood the market he was eventually forced to abandon his greeting-card publishing business.

Early Christmas cards were small, the size of visiting cards, with embossed borders and die-stamped with seasonal greetings. As demand grew printers began to adapt their paper lace Valentines for Christmas and New Year cards. Germany was the centre of excellence for printing techniques in the mid-nineteenth century, and many cards bearing the names of English publishers were printed in Bavaria and, from the mid 1870s, the unified country Germany. Many printers had businesses in England, America and Germany and the finest German cards were printed for Raphael Tuck who, in 1880, initiated the idea of Christmas card competitions offering monetary prizes. In the same year, Louis Prang organized a competition for Christmas card designs with prizes of up to $1,000 being awarded.

The introduction of the postcard in 1894 spelt the demise of the Christmas card. Postcards were a uniform size, they were inexpensive to print, to purchase and to send, and the range of subjects was vast. Interest in the Christmas card did not revive until after the First World War.

Most examples of Victorian cards are now in private collections and museums. The subjects are wide-ranging and a valuable source of social history, providing us with a picture of the social attitudes and everyday life of ordinary people often overlooked by historians dealing with more prominent national events.

MATERIALS AND EQUIPMENT

The materials and equipment for making mechanical cards are few and inexpensive and available from most craft shops. Below is a list of essential, useful and decorative equipment. Each project lists the specific items needed for that particular card.

ESSENTIAL

Card
Card is sold by its weight, known as gsm (grammes per square metre). 160 gsm is appropriate for most types of movable cards and was used for the mechanisms featured in this book. It is firm, easy to fold and suitable for use with most home printers. For outer cards where the mechanism is heavier and requires to be held firmly 210–240gsm may be used.

Graph paper and tracing paper
Graph paper with 5mm squares is used to correctly align images horizontally and vertically in card apertures. Tracing paper is used to accurately mark the placement of slots in three-dimensional découpage-style cards. Tracing paper is also useful for determining the position of images in relation to the whole picture; for instance, on stages and in windows.

Masking tape
Use low-tack masking tape to temporarily hold sections together during card construction, as ordinary masking tape will lift the surface of coloured paper and card. Always check first by testing the masking tape on a scrap piece of printed card.

Glue
Poly Vinyl Acetate (PVA) is a white water-based glue that becomes transparent when dry. Stainless-steel fine glue applicators are available to fit the top of plastic glue bottles and enable tiny spots of glue to be applied. Keep the glue bottle inverted when not in use to prevent a film forming round the tip of the nozzle.

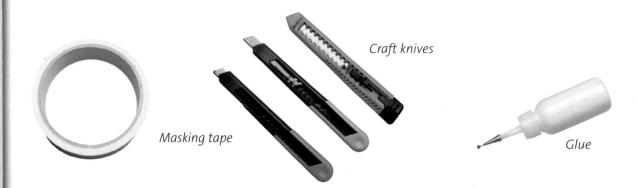

Craft knives

Masking tape

Glue

Craft knife
Paper and card quickly blunt knife blades and it is essential to maintain a crisp cutting edge. The most suitable knife is one that has a retractable strip of snap-off blades, the length of which can be locked into one of several positions on the non-slip handle.

Wire
Beading wire or cotton-covered sugar flower wire is used to hold mechanisms together. Both types of wire are available in various thicknesses. No. 24 is a standard gauge wire for paper engineering. Avoid using very fine wire, as there is a tendency for the wire to cut through the card and prevent the mechanism from functioning smoothly.

Cutting mat
Self-healing mats are made from a composite vinyl material and provide a durable non-slip surface for repetitive cutting. They are available in assorted sizes from A6 to A1 and are suitable for both straight and rotary blades. Guidelines are printed on one side of the mat to assist accurate cutting.

Rulers
Steel rulers come in various lengths. They are printed with both metric and imperial measurements and this item of equipment is essential when cutting with a craft knife. Some have a non-slip cork backing to prevent slippage but small strips of sandpaper applied to the back will produce the same effect. A flexible transparent ruler is recommended for all other use.

Scissors
Use steel scissors with short, straight blades and pointed tips that have been made specifically for cutting paper and card. Paper quickly blunts the blades and it is wise to invest in good-quality scissors.

Pencil
An automatic pencil with a 0.5mm or 0.7mm lead is recommended. This type of pencil produces a fine, accurate line and has an eraser at the end.

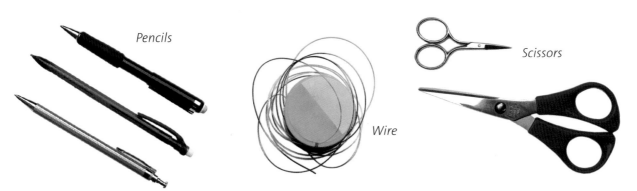

Pencils

Wire

Scissors

Scorer

Traditionally associated with book binding, bone folders are used to make sharp creases in paper and card and for burnishing edges. The folder is drawn along the edge of the steel ruler to give an indentation in the card, resulting in a sharp edge when the card is folded. Folders sold in craft shops are generally made from plastic. Equally effective for scoring are the tips of used biros and knitting needles (particularly cable needles, which come in a range of sizes). Score using the pointed end and burnish by laying the needle on its side.

Push pins

The type of pin used to secure memos to a corkboard is ideal for piercing holes in card and is the correct size for threading through the wire required to hold mechanisms together.

USEFUL

Circle cutter

Circles are extremely difficult to cut freehand and there are several cutters available to assist with this task. The cutter pictured below is based on a pair of compasses and will cut circles up to ⅝in (1.5cm) diameter. It comes supplied with spare blades and pencil leads which are stored in the handle and will cut through paper, leather, vinyl, etc. The cutter shown on the left has a clear base and the adjustable arm enables the user to cut circles from ⅝–8in (1.5–20cm) with the option of using a gripper foot to eliminate a hole in the centre of the circle.

Cork mat

A thick cork table mat is perfect for pricking through holes in templates. Pin mechanisms to the cork mat to check that the movement is functioning correctly before permanently fixing parts together with wire. Larger cork boards are obtainable from lace suppliers. Cork tiles can be used but two should be glued together to give sufficient depth for the pricking.

Mini paper fasteners

Mini paper fasteners (also known as brads) can sometimes be used as an alternative to wire for holding rotary mechanisms in place. They are available in various sizes, shapes and colours.

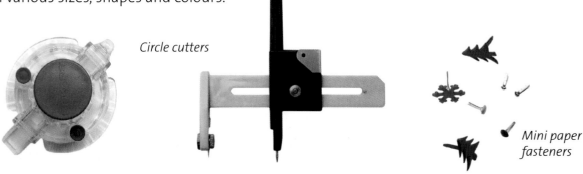

Circle cutters

Mini paper fasteners

Eyelet punch
These are available in assorted sizes ranging from ⅛in (3mm). They are operated by placing the punch in the required position and hammering. An advanced setter is also available – the tension can be adjusted for punching softer card by twisting the handle.

Spray-on adhesive
This is effective when gluing designs cut from wrapping paper to cartridge paper.

Mini pliers
These are used to cut the wire and to pull it tightly around a thin cable needle to make wire rivets.

Linen thread
This is used to sew the segments together in the Pull-tab Fan project on page 88. The thread used in this project should be fairly strong and blend with the colour used for the back of the fan segments.

DECORATIVE
Paper punches
There is a wide range of punches for cutting decorative shapes, either through the card or for making designs to apply to the card. The most useful of these are circle-cutting punches, ⅝in and 1in (1.5cm and 2.5cm) wide, which are perfect for covering wire ends to prevent them from damaging paper and card.

Paper edge scissors
Used to create decorative edges to card and paper, these are available in a variety of designs.

Wrapping paper
Examine your wrapping paper carefully before discarding it to the waste collection – it is an excellent design source for card makers. Cut pictures out and store them in a design folder for reference when required. Photocopy or scan selected areas or mount the required illustration on cartridge paper to stiffen and then use for your card.

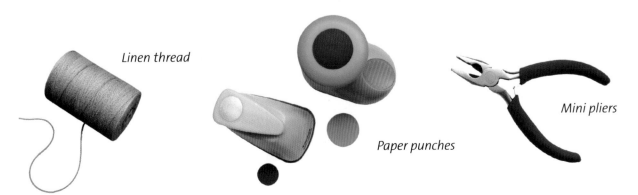

Linen thread

Paper punches

Mini pliers

Stickers

Stickers add a professional look to cards. There is a large selection available in a variety of materials catering for all hobbies and interests. Some are dimensional and others peel-off scraps.

Découpage paper

Paper sold for three-dimensional découpage is useful for the 90° Variation card (see page 42), especially where flowers are the focal point.

Rubber stamps

These come in various sizes, and most stockists have catalogues from which further designs can be selected. Designs can be stamped and hand-coloured or stamped using special pads which have a striation of colours. Illustrations of stamps in some catalogues are copyright free and, after scanning, can be reduced or enlarged. Stamps are recommended for filling large areas, particularly around dissolving pictures as the patterns merge into the background and do not detract from the aperture.

Paper and card

Available in different weights and colours, special paper and card effects include holograms, patterns, corrugated, metallic and textured.

Foam

Thin foam shapes are easily cut with scissors and give added dimension to cards.

Fabric

Patchwork suppliers have a vast stock of designs which include small prints suitable for card-making. Cut out the required section leaving an allowance round the edge. Mount the fabric on to card using iron-on adhesives, which require only a low temperature.

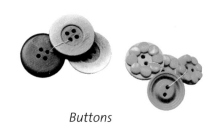

Fabric

Buttons

Scraps
Reproductions of 19th-century German scraps are available in sheets. These are embossed and have a high gloss.

Lace
Paper doilies are manufactured in a variety of shapes and sizes. Reproduction 19th-century lace cards are available from some craft outlets. Lace border and corner punches are effective, and punch shapers allow lace designs to be placed on any part of the card. Embossing tools have smooth, rounded tips and are used with brass stencils to work selected areas.

Haberdashery
Ribbons, buttons, lace, paper flowers, paper-covered wire, beads, sequins and many other card-making items can be purchased inexpensively from market stalls, supermarkets, florists and department stores.

Other design sources
Internet: Access to a computer will provide the card-maker with a wealth of source material. Many sites allow free use of downloaded material.

Magazines and books: Colour magazines are an easily accessed source, and pictures can be scanned or photocopied. Designs cut directly from magazines should be spray mounted on to cartridge paper to stiffen them. Children's books are a wonderful source of material, particularly coloured picture books.

Specialist catalogues: Gift catalogues and garden catalogues are often inspirational. Cut out possible designs and save them in your file.

Greetings cards: Before discarding greetings cards, check to see if anything can be reused in your designs.

Photocopying: Colour photocopies are inexpensive. To save time, mount several designs on an A4 piece of paper and photocopy two or three sheets. Keep the originals for future reference.

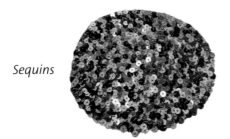

Sequins

Important:
Always check for copyright on designs you intend to use for commercial purposes.

TECHNIQUES

Before you begin

Test each template before cutting into expensive card. Photocopy or transfer the templates (see below) to cartridge paper or waste card and assemble the pieces following the step-by-step instructions, diagrams and any additional hints. If your mechanism fails to work, look carefully at the instructions and check that a piece has not been glued upside down, or that the pull-tab was placed incorrectly when fastening the pieces together.

Starting a card

Once you have tested the instructions and followed them correctly, take your chosen card (see page 14 for advice on choosing card) and transfer the templates as described below.

The templates indicate the size of card required to conceal the mechanism and allow the object to be viewed in the aperture. Background card must be cut three times the width of the template: the mechanism and picture appear in the centre, the right side covers the mechanism and the message is written on the left side. Alternatively, you could cut only the front and back of the card then glue a larger piece of card to the inside front. Ensure that the mechanism is not impeded by applying glue only to the outer edges. When dry, the excess card can be removed.

Transferring templates

For straight lines, place the template on the card and prick through the points to be joined. Remove the paper and, using a ruler, join up the dots.

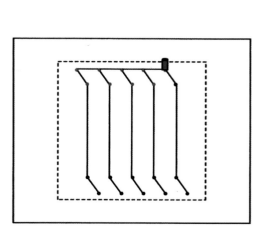 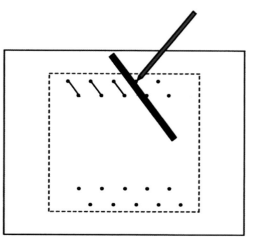

Place the template on the card and prick through the points to be joined. Remove the paper and join up the dots.

For curved lines, place the template on the card and prick points through the curves ¹⁄₁₆–¹⁄₈in (2–3mm) apart. Remove the paper and join up the dots. For large curved areas use the compass method described below.

Place the template on the card and prick points through the curves ¹⁄₁₆–¹⁄₈in (2–3mm) apart. Remove the paper and join up the dots. For large curved areas use the compass method described below.

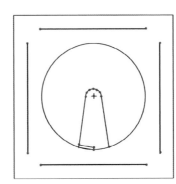
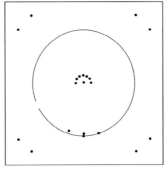

Decoration

Apart from the Puzzle Purse on page 28, all decoration should be done before cutting the card. The instructions assume that the card has been suitably decorated prior to making up.

Scoring the card

Dotted lines on the templates indicate an area to be scored, folded and creased. Before beginning the instructions for a project, score any dotted lines with a bone folder, cable needle or other blunt instrument.

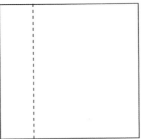

Score dotted lines, fold and crease.

Drawing and dividing circles

Draw a perfect circle with a standard pair of compasses or make your own from a strip of card. Pierce a point at one end and further points at the required radius length. The strip is positioned on the card then pinned to the cork board. Place the automatic pencil point through the radius hole and draw a circle. This method ensures a perfect circle as the pencil is held at 90 degrees to the card, thus preventing distortion of the central hole by the point of the compasses.

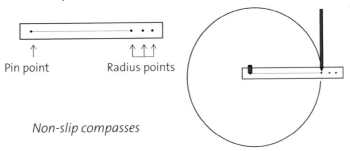

Pin point   Radius points

Non-slip compasses

To accurately divide a circle into segments first draw it inside a square. Mark a line across the centre of the square and mark off the required segments using a protractor.

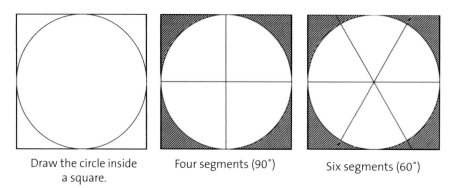

Draw the circle inside a square.

Four segments (90°)

Six segments (60°)

Dividing a circle into sections.

Making up

It is essential to test the templates first to familiarize yourself with the instructions. Thin card from the back of cereal packets is useful for this purpose. Testing the templates will enable you to see exactly how the mechanism fits together and avoid the disappointment of wasting expensive materials.

Cutting the card

Areas to be cut are illustrated on the templates by solid lines and areas to be removed are shaded. Sharp corners may impede mechanisms and should be rounded off.

Remove sharp corners.

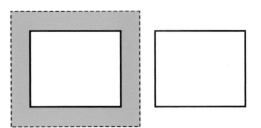

Cut out along solid lines.

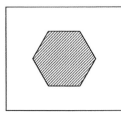

Remove shaded areas.

With scissors
Feed paper through your scissors as you cut, rather than moving the blades through the paper. Avoid cutting to the tips of the blades as this will result in a rough edge.

With a craft knife
Always use a steel ruler when cutting straight lines with a craft knife. Draw the knife blade towards you in the same way that a pencil would be used to draw a margin down a page. Several light strokes will cut easily through thick card but pressure on the knife will result in a ragged edge.

Cutting out small areas
Paper is extremely strong when in a solid piece; therefore small sections should always be removed first before cutting around the outline. Make a slit in the centre of the piece to be removed and feed one of the scissor blades through the slit from underneath.

Push one blade of the scissors through the slit from underneath the design.

Slide the blades to the end of the slit and begin to remove the shaded area by feeding the paper through the scissors.

Slots are cut to allow pull-tabs and mechanisms to move freely. Note that these are wider than a 'slit', which is a single cut through a card. All slots should be removed prior to cutting round the template.

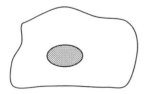

Shaded section to be removed.

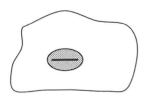

Using a craft knife, make a slit in the centre of the shaded area.

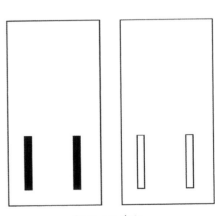

Remove slots.

Cutting circles

A craft knife can be used to cut circles. Rather than try to follow the outline of a circle with your knife, which can result in tears or a jagged edge, it is advisable to hold your craft knife steady and move the paper in a circular action.

However, a circle cutter will give you the best results. Make sure you tighten the circle-cutter screw with pliers first to reduce the risk of 'slippage'. To prevent the centre enlarging when using the circle cutter, place a small piece of folded masking tape between the hole position and a cork mat. Circles are accurately cut by pinning the card to a cork mat with the circumference of the circle slightly protruding from the edge of the mat. Keeping the cutter stationary, move the card round the circle cutter and not the cutter round the card. Applying pressure to the circle cutter will distort the centre hole and result in an unsatisfactory aperture.

Cutting figures and scenery

Do not cut precisely round each shape: a general smooth outline is more professional and will allow moving parts to slide easily. Temper the edges of cut sections by burnishing with a bone folder or a cable needle. White edges can be softened using a suitably coloured pencil.

Include part of the background when cutting out shapes to avoid sharp corners and points which may crease and impede the smooth movement of the mechanism.

Piercing holes

A push pin is perfect for piercing holes in the cards. Always rest your card on a cork board when piercing holes.

Folding

Always fold inwards towards the scored line, burnishing the creased edge with a bone folder or the side of a cable needle.

Gluing

The small shaded areas on tabs are glue spots. Ensure that glue is only applied to the centre of the tab, as any leakage to the surrounding area will result in the mechanism failing to function correctly.

Apply glue spots to shaded areas on tabs.

Aligning figures in apertures

To align figures horizontally in an aperture, arrange them in the correct position on graph paper and fix lightly in place with masking tape. Using the graph paper, rule a line across the ground level. Add the required tab height.

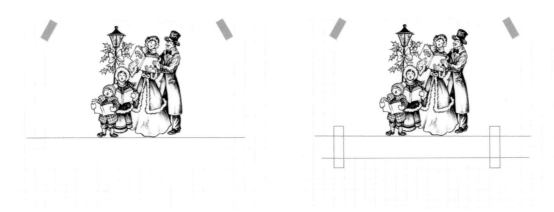

*Align the picture correctly on the graph paper and hold in place with masking tape.
Rule a line below the picture using the graph paper as a guide. Use the graph paper lines
as a guide to draw a stand and tabs at either end of the picture.*

*Cut around the
picture and tabs.*

THE MECHANICAL CARDS

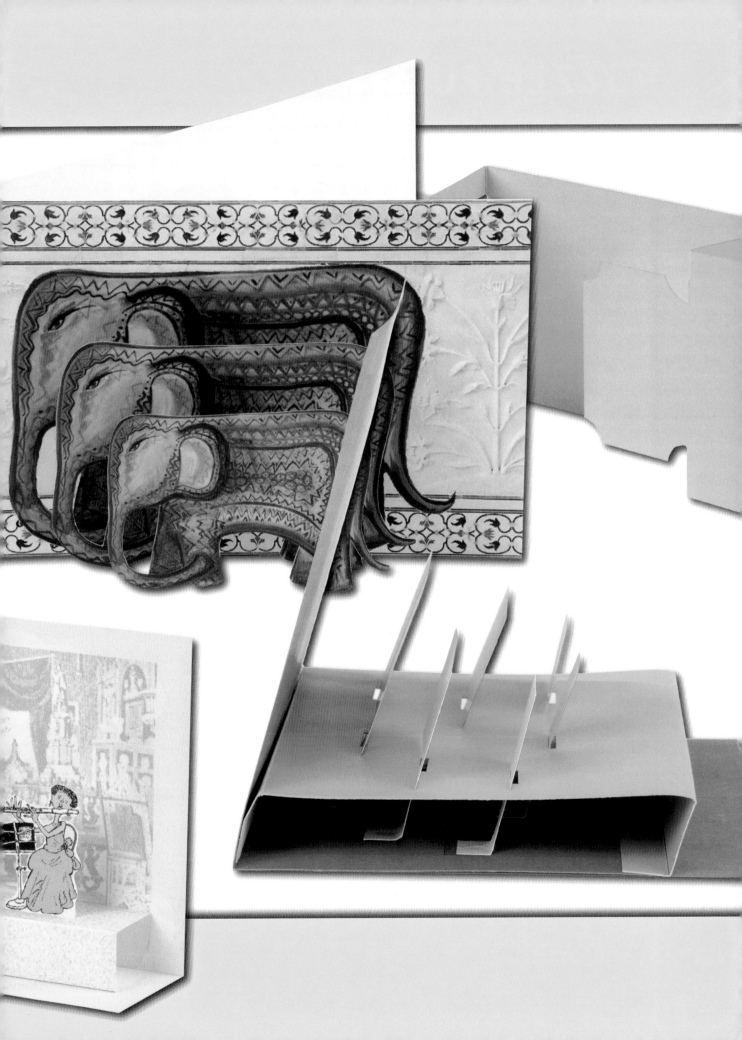

PUZZLE PURSE

Early novelty Valentines included Puzzle Purses: squares of paper folded origami-style with messages written inside them. When completely unfolded it was difficult to read the messages they contained, hence their name. Early examples were handmade and sometimes contained a flower cage (see page 34), a lock of hair or another token of sentiment in the centre. As envelopes were unavailable until the mid 19th century, puzzle purses were sealed on the back with wax and the recipient's name and address were written on the front.

1 Fold the template into three horizontally and vertically.

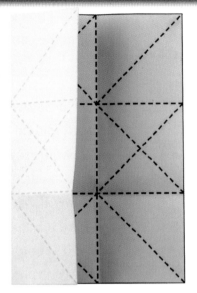

2 Fold the template diagonally both ways and crease each corner avoiding the central square which should remain flat.

3 Fold each corner across the central square and then crease.

MATERIALS
- **Template on page 122** transferred on to paper
- Bone folder
- Coloured pens, pencils or paints

4 Pinch the corners together to form a box shape around the central square.

5 Press the lower triangles in each middle square downwards towards the central square. The puzzle should collapse on itself and the top tips of the triangles should meet in the central square.

6 Fold each flap across the centre, inserting the fourth flap under the first flap to secure.

7 Decorate the finished, folded square with a picture. The name and address of the sender can be written on the reverse side of the folded square if desired (this is a complete square, no folds).

8 Unfold the flaps and write lines of prose on the next layer.

9 Open the purse up fully and decorate any remaining triangles with pictures.

10 Refold the purse.

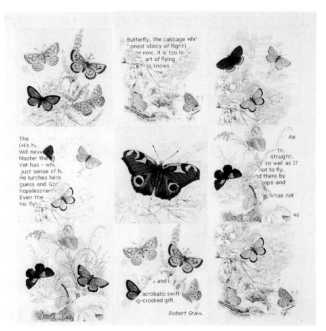

PAPER SPRINGS

Paper springs were the result of an early attempt to create three-dimensional cards; they were used during the mid 19th century to separate layers of paper lace on Valentine cards. Strips of thin cardboard were folded accordion style and inserted between sheets of paper lace which were then raised manually. This allowed the layers to stand away from each other and form a three-dimensional effect. Paper springs were also placed under applied fabric to give a similar effect to clothed figures when the fabric was raised.

1 Use graph paper as a guide to divide the strips of card into equal sections, then crease and accordion fold to form paper springs. Attach one end to the backing card and the other end to the picture to be pulled forward. *Note:* Two paper springs will provide added stability and are essential for supporting larger images.

2 Use a tab of glue to attach one shaded end to the backing card and the other shaded end to the front card.

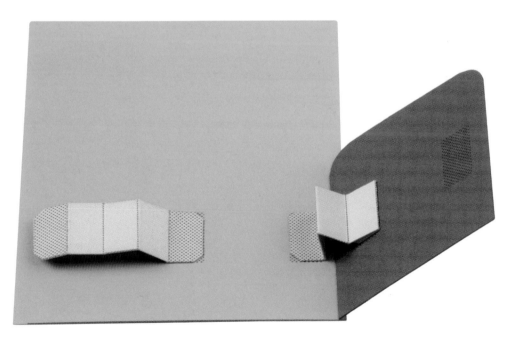

MATERIALS

- **Templates on page 123** transferred on to card
- Graph paper
- Bone folder
- Glue

PAPER CAGE

Paper cages were also referred to as 'Beehives', 'Cobwebs' and 'Flower Cages'. The paper cage is operated by pulling a piece of thread attached to its centre which lifts to reveal a message or token of sentiment, such as a lock of hair. Paper-cage cutting was a skilful task, the cuts being less than $\frac{1}{16}$in (2mm) apart. It required special training and was rewarded with additional payment. Initial attempts should be tested using a large template.

1 Lay the template copy on to your selected image and hold in place with masking tape.

2 Commencing in the centre of the cage, cut along the solid lines with a craft knife and use a pin to pierce a hole in the centre (marked with a cross on the template).

3 Remove the masking tape and the template copy. Use a bone folder, or similar, to burnish across the cut lines to smooth the edges.

4 Fasten a piece of thread through the pierced hole in the centre by tying a knot and applying a spot of glue to prevent the thread slipping through the hole.

5 If your chosen image is part of a larger design that you do not wish to include on your card, you should cut it out now from the background.

6 Prepare the card front, placing a design to appear under the cage, e.g. rubber stamp, scrap or design cut from wrapping paper.

7 Finally, glue the edges of the cage to the front of the card, placing the centre over the design to appear when the thread is pulled up.

MATERIALS

- **Template on page 124** (choice of round or rectangular) transferred on to plain paper
- Printed image to form the cage
- Printed image to be revealed behind the cage
- Background card
- Masking tape
- Scissors
- Pin (to pierce hole)
- Bone folder
- Thread
- Glue

SLIDE MECHANISM

This mechanism is cut in one piece from the card and is slotted from the front to the back, allowing the image to slide across when the card is opened. It is advisable to use a heavy card for this mechanism – double thickness 240gsm is ideal.

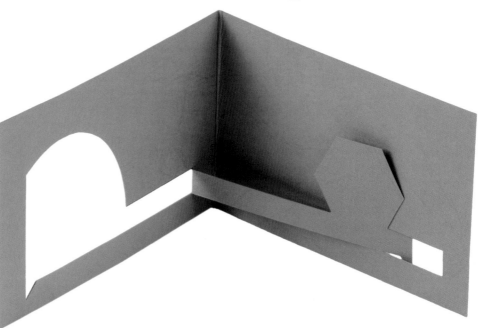

1 Score the centre crease and fold the card in half.

2 Score the pull-tab fold.

3 Remove the aperture from the back of the card.

4 Cut along the solid lines on the pull-tab.

5 Remove the shaded area.

6 Refold the card and slot the pull-tab into the aperture on the back.

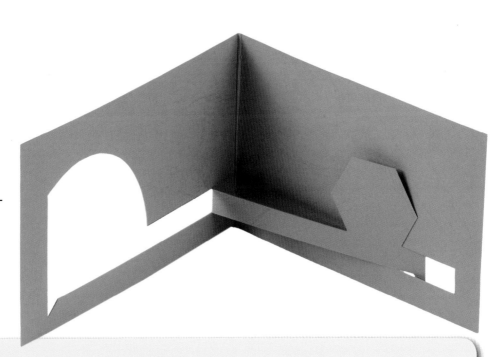

MATERIALS
- **Template on page 125** transferred on to heavy card
- Bone folder
- Craft knife

ACCORDION FOLD

Accordion folds are cut from a single piece of
card. The principle of the accordion fold is to cut
partly round a shape and to fold the surplus card away
from the shape to give a dimensional effect. As the image
is cut directly from the card it does not require glue to maintain its
position. It is the most inexpensive method of mass-producing three-
dimensional pictures and is extensively used in pop-up books.

1 Score the dotted lines.

2 Cut along the solid lines.

3 Use a craft knife to remove the shaded areas.

4 Accordion fold to the centre on the scored lines.

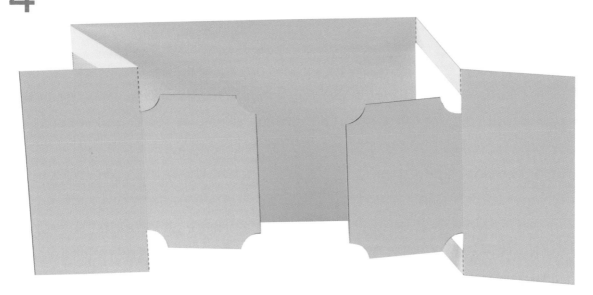

MATERIALS
- **Template on page 126** transferred on to card
- Bone folder
- Scissors
- Craft knife

90° BASIC CARD

The printer and stationer Dean, established in the 1830s, was the first to introduce three-dimensional pictures. The early cards had scenes which were fastened together with linen thread, later ones with small strips of paper. This mechanism dates back to the mid 19th century when Dean first included the idea in his *Transformation* series of books. The original design had layers which were glued along the top of the page and folded flat inside the book. To operate the mechanism a thread was attached to the back layer which, when pulled, allowed the front layers to stand at 90 degrees to the base of the book. This was a popular mechanism for animated Christmas cards. There is no limit to the number of scenes, each one being connected either to the background or to another scene.

1 Score, fold, crease and cut out the background card.

2 Draw ⅜in (1cm) tab placement lines on the back of each scene as follows:
  scene 1: ¹³⁄₁₆in (2.5cm) above the scene tab fold
  scenes 2 and 3: ⅝in (1.5cm) above the scene tab fold.

3 Score and fold the scene tabs and glue them to the marked positions on the background card.

4 Fold the tabs on the numbered strips and glue one end of them to the corresponding scene where marked.

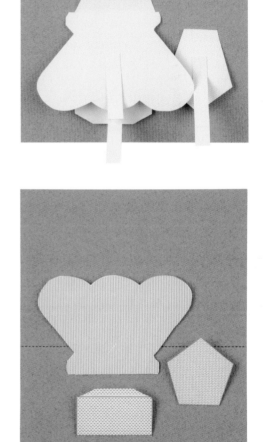

5 Apply a spot of glue to the tab on scene 1. Glue scene 1 to the top half of the background card. Press firmly and allow to dry. *Note:* Use only a small spot of glue to attach the tabs to the background card. This will allow the length of the strips to adjust if necessary when closing the background card. There may be a slight variation in the length depending on the thickness of card used to make the strips. Repeat with scenes 2 and 3.

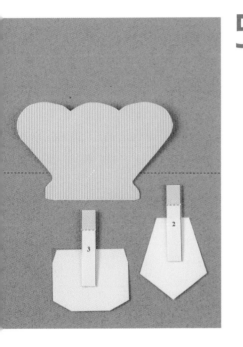

MATERIALS
- **Templates on page 127,** transferred on to card
- Bone folder
- Glue
- Scissors

90° VARIATION

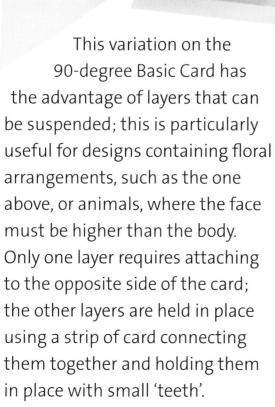

This variation on the 90-degree Basic Card has the advantage of layers that can be suspended; this is particularly useful for designs containing floral arrangements, such as the one above, or animals, where the face must be higher than the body. Only one layer requires attaching to the opposite side of the card; the other layers are held in place using a strip of card connecting them together and holding them in place with small 'teeth'.

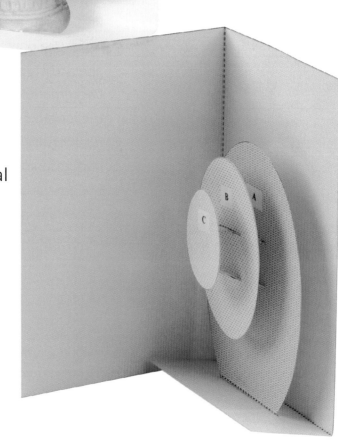

1 Score, fold, crease and then cut out the background card.

2 Score the fold on A and remove the slots from A and B using a craft knife. Cut out A and B.

3 Score the dotted lines on the stand, fold, crease and then cut out. Fold back the 'teeth'.

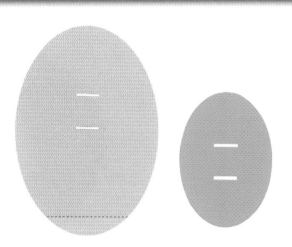

4 From the front of B, insert the stand through the slots.

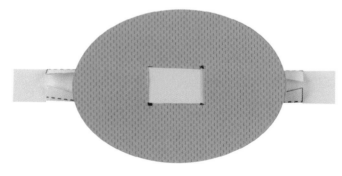

Front   *Back*

MATERIALS
- **Templates on pages 128** transferred on to card
- Bone folder
- Scissors
- Craft knife
- Glue

5 Glue C to the centre of the stand.

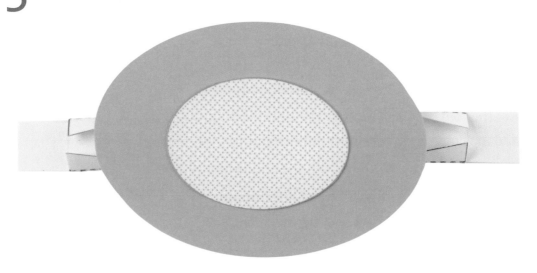

6 Open the 'teeth' to separate B and C. Thread the stand through A.

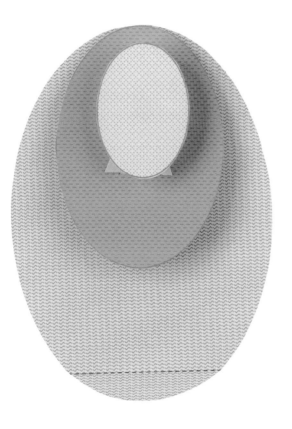

7 Fold the mechanism with the top layer facing upwards. Turn the mechanism over and fold the top tab upwards.

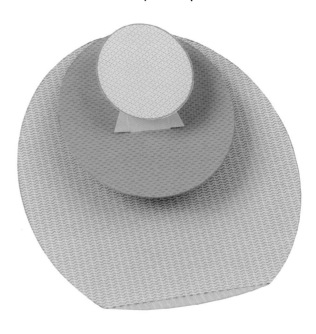

8 Glue the tab on A to the marked position on the card and allow to dry.

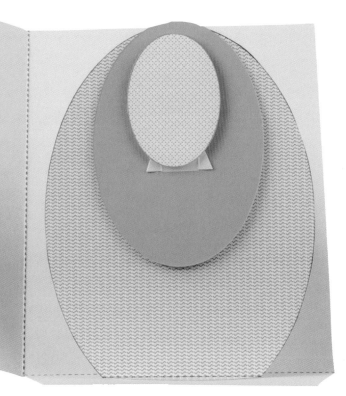

9 Apply glue spots to the stand tabs.

10 Bring the flap up, close the card then press the glued tabs firmly to the back of the card. Allow to dry before opening.

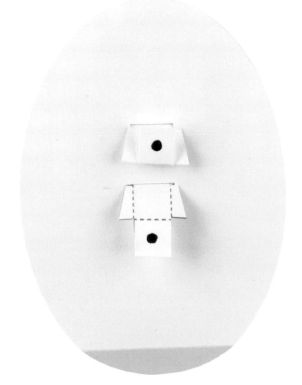

90° BOX STAGE

The figures or scenes in this card are held upright by passing them through slots and gluing them to the base of the card. This gives them the appearance of being free-standing.

1 Score and fold the centre of the backing card.

2 Score and fold the dotted lines in the stage. Remove the slots.

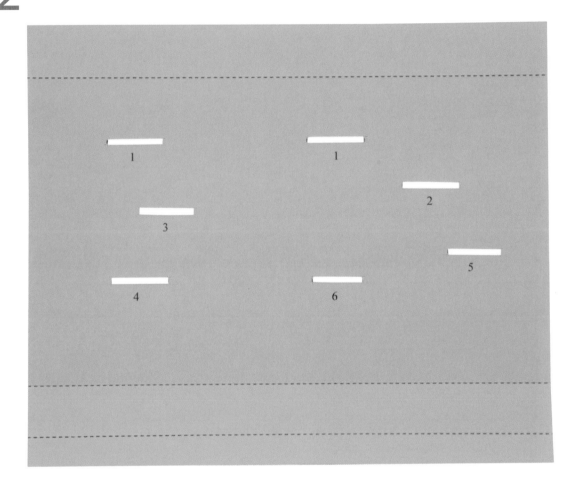

MATERIALS

- **Templates on pages 129–130** transferred on to card
- Figures for stage
- Masking tape
- Bone folder
- Scissors
- Craft knife
- Glue

3 Score the fold lines on the figure tabs. Cut out the figure tabs and crease firmly on the scored tab lines. Open out flat.

4 Glue the back tab of the stage to the backing card, aligning the cut edge with the centre fold.

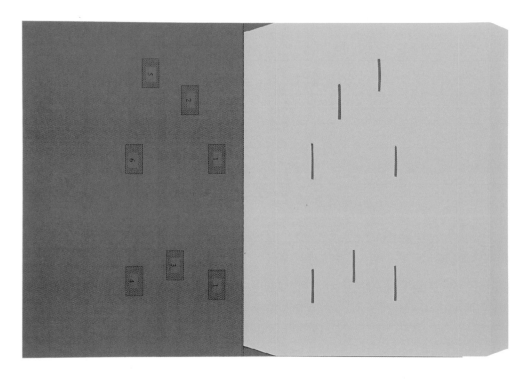

5 Starting with the back figure, insert the tabs through the appropriate slots. If necessary, keep them in place with low-tack masking tape before gluing them. Fold down the front stage on the first dotted line.

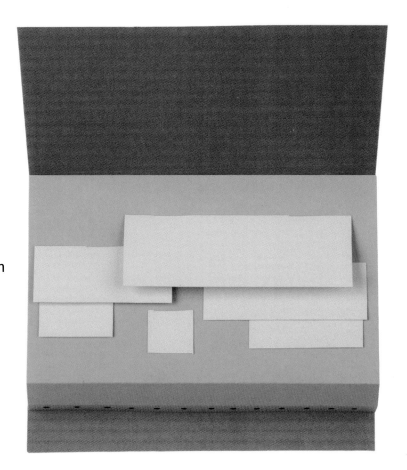

6 Apply glue to the tabs and along the edge of the front stage. Carefully fold up the backing card and glue firmly to the stage front and figure tabs. Allow the glue to dry before opening the card.

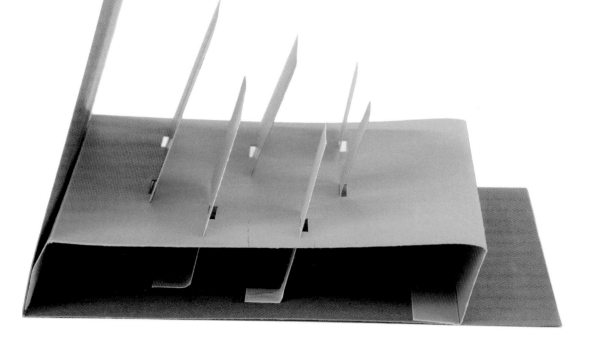

90° SLEEVE STAGE

The mechanism required to raise this card is cut from a separate card and glued to the back of a moving image. A card sleeve is wrapped around the moving image and mechanism and then slid upwards, causing the image to fold at 90 degrees and allowing it to free-stand. The card has a further dimensional scene using the method described for the 90-degree Basic Card (see page 40) but in this instance the glued tab has been inserted through a slot in the moving image and pasted to the back.

1 Cut out, score and crease the folds on all the templates.

2 Insert the stand tab through the short slot in the sleeve and the picture tab through the long slot and glue both to the back of the sleeve.

MATERIALS

- **Templates on page 131** transferred on to card
- Glue
- Scissors
- Craft knife
- Masking tape
- Bone folder

3 Apply a spot of glue on the stand tab and glue the dimensional picture in place. *Note:* The glue must not spread beyond the edges of the small tab.

4 Place the sleeve on the card back, aligning the lower edges and the centre. Hold in place with masking tape and turn over to the wrong side.

5 Score the sliding mechanism at either side of the sleeve and fold the flaps over the backing card. Check that the sleeve will slide easily – it may be necessary to score further away from the edges. Glue the flaps to complete the sleeve.

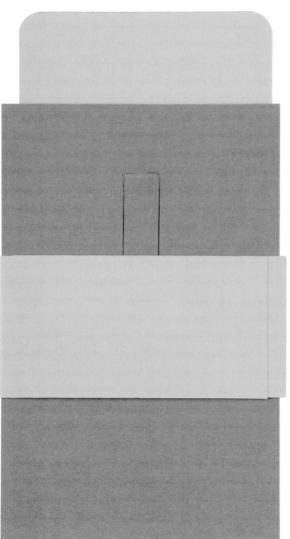

6 Apply a glue spot to the tab on the card back where indicated and attach to the sleeve. *Note: The glue must not spread beyond the edges of the small tab or the mechanism will be prevented from sliding. Remove the masking tape.*

90° WIDE PULL-TAB STAGE

This design has a wide tab that is pulled down to reveal a three-dimensional stage in the aperture. The scenes are attached to supports at the top and bottom of the stage to keep them upright when the card is opened. Glue the sides of the card together sparingly along the extreme outer edges, ensuring that the pull-tab has sufficient space in which to move freely.

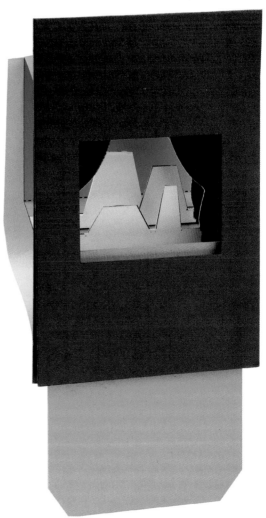

1 Score, fold and crease along the dotted lines on the templates before cutting round the solid lines. Open out each section flat.

2 Cut the slot on the pull-tab wide enough to accommodate the width of the ribbon.

3 Cut the ribbon slot on the card. Fold the card and cut the aperture through both layers (see Notes on page 59). Open the card.

MATERIALS
- **Templates on pages 132–133** transferred on to card
- Bone folder
- Scissors
- Craft knife
- Ribbon
- Masking tape

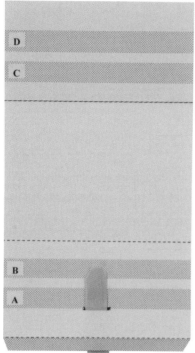

4 Cut the ribbon slot in the stage and pass through the end of the ribbon. Glue and secure with masking tape.

5 Make the stage and scenery/figures. The scenery/figures are set into frames to ensure they stand upright on the stage. To attach the scenery frames glue in the following order:
i) lower edge of the back scene
ii) lower edge of the front scene.

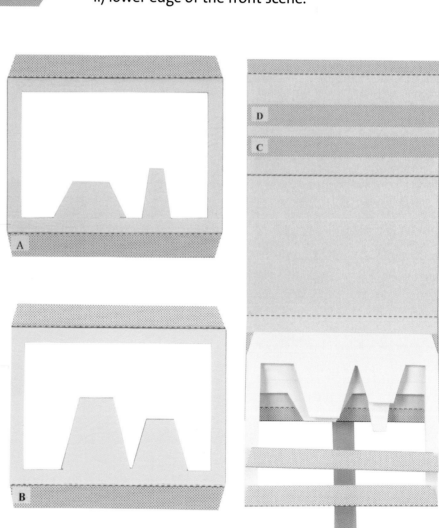

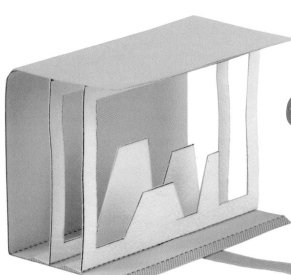

6 The lower stage should be folded up and glue applied to the top scenery tabs. Press firmly to the top stage.

7 Glue the stage on to the marked positions above and below the aperture. Fold and crease the stage towards the top of the card. Pull the end of the ribbon through the slot in the card.

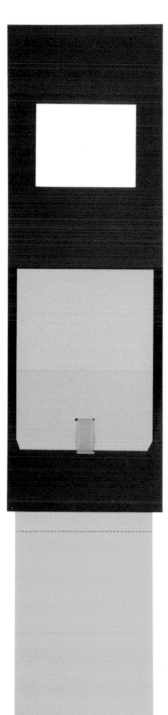

8 Pull the end of the ribbon through the slot in the pull-tab.

9 Align the top of the pull-tab with the top of the aperture and hold in place temporarily with masking tape. Pull up any slack in the ribbon, glue to the tab, securing with a small piece of masking tape and cut off the excess ribbon. Fold up the pull-tab in half and glue to conceal the ribbon.

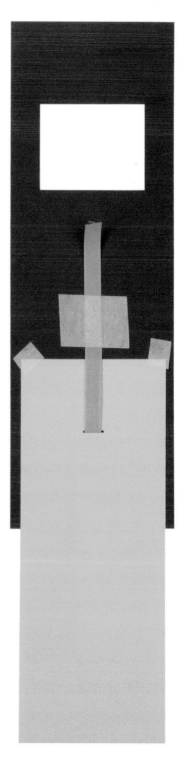

10 Glue carriers either side of it to allow it to move up and down smoothly. Fold down the front of the card and, avoiding the pull-tab, glue the sides together.

11 To finish, glue a piece of paper to the top of the stage and the bottom of the card.

NOTES
There are two methods of removing the aperture in the centre of the stage card:

Method 1
1. Fold and crease the card.
2. Place on a cork mat and prick through the corners with a push pin. The blade will stop when it hits the indentation and the panel will come out cleanly.

Method 2
1. Cut the aperture from the card front first.
2. Fold the card and trace the inside of the aperture.
3. Open the card and cut the second aperture slightly larger.

90° PAPER SPRING VARIATION

In this design two cards are separated by paper springs. A wide tab passes through a slot in the front card on which a figure/scene is mounted. The mechanism is operated by pulling the front card forward on the paper springs to raise the figure/scene from the background card in the aperture.

1 Cut out all the templates, score all dotted lines, remove the slot from the front card and remove the aperture.

2 Fold the lower edge of the outer oval and glue to the inner oval, avoiding the small folded area.

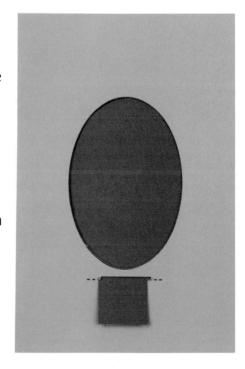

3 Prepare the paper springs (see step 1, page 33) and glue to the edges of the backing card.

4 Insert the inner oval tab through the slot in the outer card.

MATERIALS
- **Templates on page 134** transferred on to card
- Scissors
- Craft knife
- Glue

5 Glue the figure support to the inner oval tab.

6 Fold down the figure support (do not crease the inner oval tab) and glue the figure support tab to the front of the card.

7 Fold the tab and glue one end to the back of the central figure.

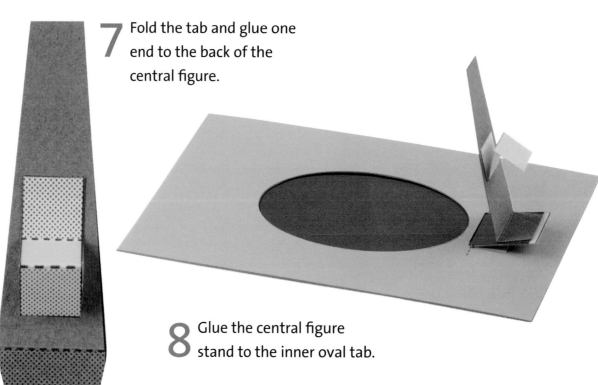

8 Glue the central figure stand to the inner oval tab.

9 Place a spot of glue on the central figure tab and glue the top card to the paper springs. Allow to dry.

10 Glue the flap on the outer oval to the front of the card.

180° BASIC CARD

This mechanism allows the card to open completely flat and each scene stands forward from the backing card. The back scene must be cut at least ⅜in (1cm) shorter than the width of the card and subsequent layers are cut ⅜in (1cm) shorter than the previous ones to ensure that the mechanism is fully enclosed in the finished card. Only the stands are shown in the templates to demonstrate how the mechanism operates. Cut out the figures/scenery in one with the stand.

1 Score the card, crease, fold and open out.

2 Score the centre of both layers, crease and fold.

3 Score the dotted lines on the stands and cut out.

4 Glue each stand into a box shape.

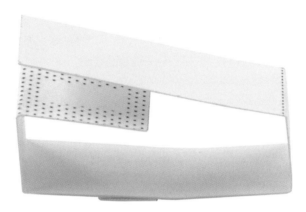

5 Glue a stand to the centre fold of the middle layer and top layer.

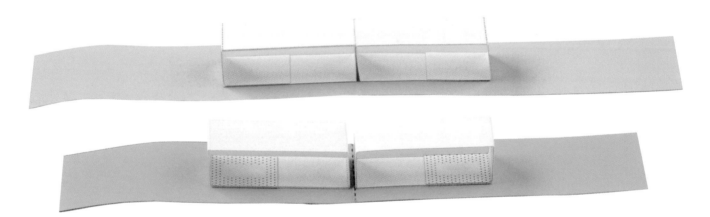

MATERIALS
- **Templates on page 135** transferred on to card
- Bone folder
- Scissors
- Glue

6 Press towards the centre fold of each layer.

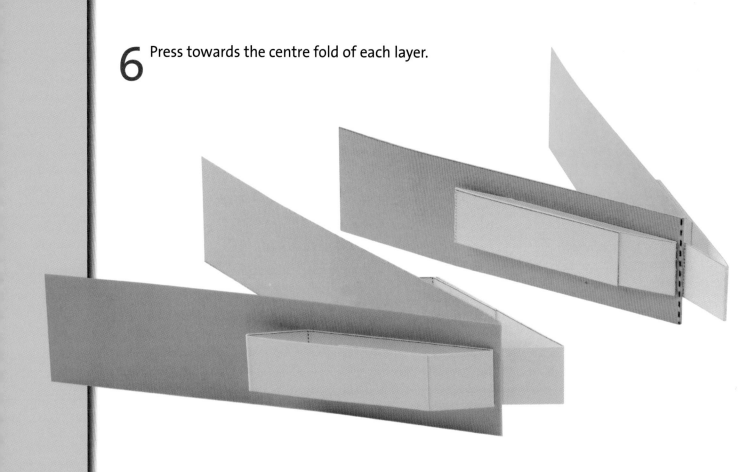

7 Glue the long edge of the middle layer back stand to the centre fold of the backing card.

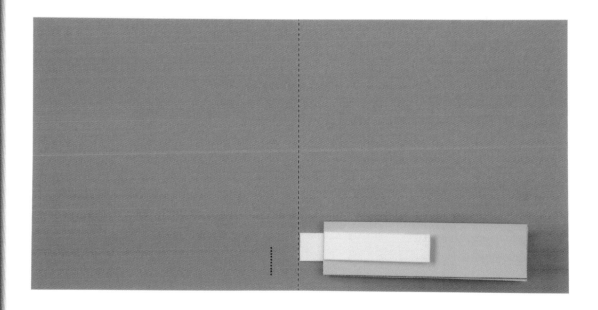

8 Glue the long edge of the top layer back stand to the centre fold of the middle layer.

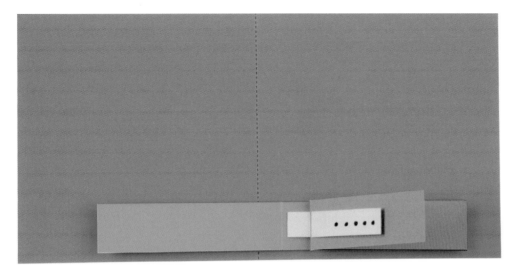

9 Push the top layer stand towards the centre fold of the middle layer.

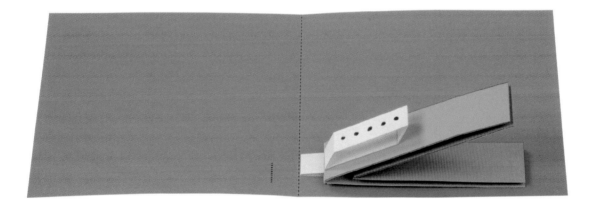

10 Apply glue to the long edge of the middle layer. Close the card and allow the glue to dry before opening.

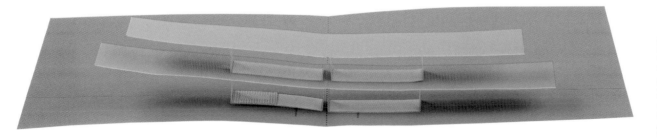

180° PEEPSHOW

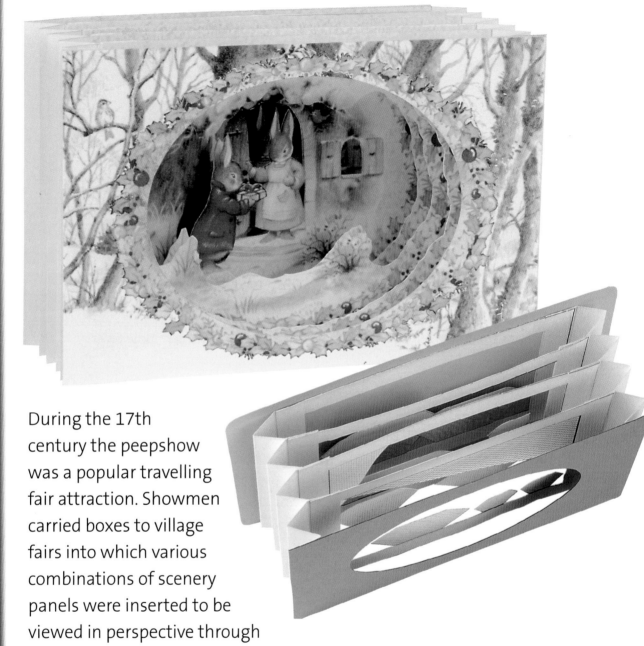

During the 17th century the peepshow was a popular travelling fair attraction. Showmen carried boxes to village fairs into which various combinations of scenery panels were inserted to be viewed in perspective through a hole in the front of the box. Many combinations of scenery were made possible by pulling up the panels with strings. By the mid 19th century printers were publishing miniature peepshows in which the scenes were separated with paper springs. These miniature peepshows often depicted major events, such as the opening of the Thames Tunnel in 1843 and the Great Exhibition 1851.

1 Score the paper springs on the dotted lines and then fold accordion style as indicated on the template.

2 Glue together the sections as shown to make holders for the frames.

MATERIALS

- **Templates on pages 136–137** transferred on to card/paper
- Contrasting background card
- Bone folder
- Glue

3 Remove the background from scenes 1, 2 and 3 (the non-shaded areas within each frame).

4 Glue one side of the background to the last folded section on one of the paper springs.

5 Glue scenes 1, 2 and 3 to the frame holders on one side.

6 Glue the background and frames to the second frame holder.

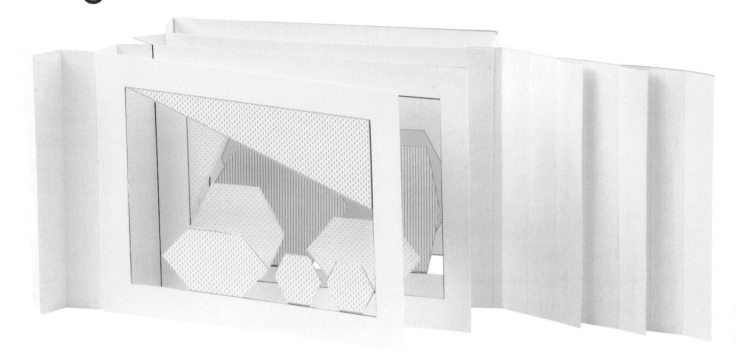

7 Glue the card front to the top of the paper spring tabs, then glue it all to a contrasting piece of card cut slightly larger than the peepshow.

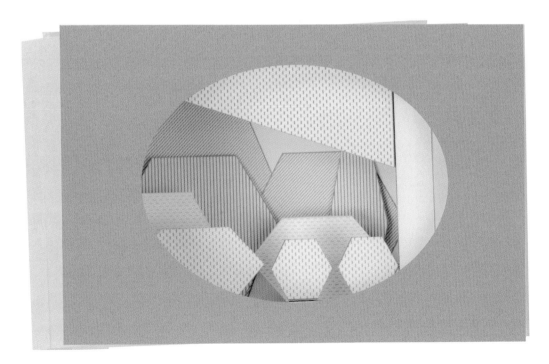

180° DOUBLE PULL-TAB STAGE

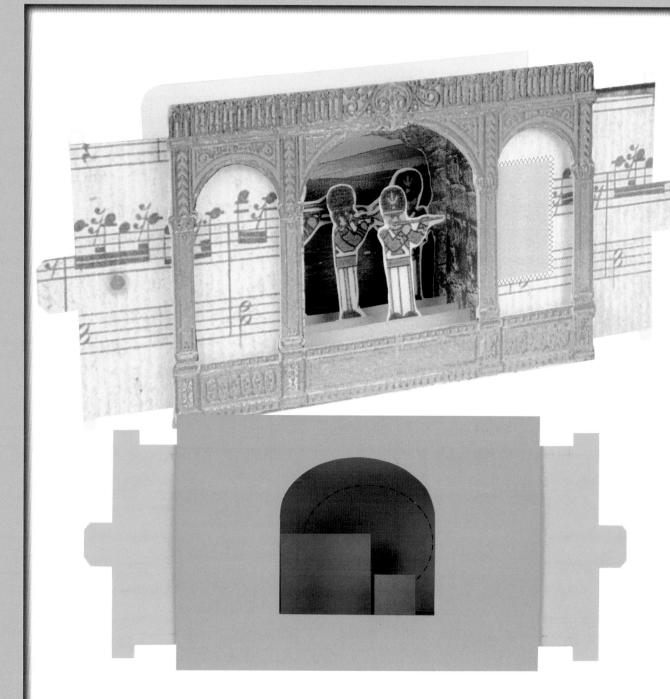

This variation on the 180-degree Basic Card is operated by pulling the two tabs on either side of the card. When opened the card is freestanding and forms a complete stage with three-dimensional scenes and a background.

1 Take the card front, score the dotted lines, fold and crease firmly.

2 Unfold the card front. Then remove the aperture and the card from the background.

3 Run glue along the creases on the scored lines and press into place.

4 Mark the position of the mechanism holders on the wrong side.

5 Take the mechanism and score all the dotted lines before cutting it out. Fold the scored lines and crease firmly.

6 Remove the slots from the side panels, run glue along the top and bottom tabs, fold and press to stiffen the side panels. *Note:* Before applying glue check that the tabs do not interfere with the cut slots – reduce the height if necessary. Cut, fold and glue the end pull-tabs.

MATERIALS
- **Templates on pages 138–139** transferred on to card
- Bone folder
- Glue
- Scissors
- Craft knife

7 Take your figures or scenery for the back stage, middle stage and front stage and glue them to their relevant stage. *Note:* The figures and scenery can be placed in any position on the stages but the card will not close if these exceed the width of the template shape. Fold and glue the lower tabs on the middle stage and front stage to strengthen them.

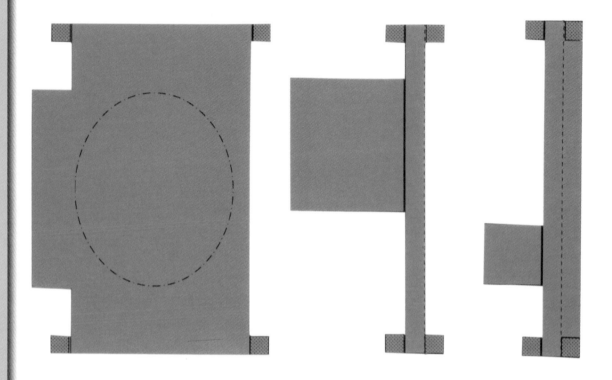

8 Fold the scenery tabs and thread them through the slots in the side panels. Complete one side first then repeat with the other.

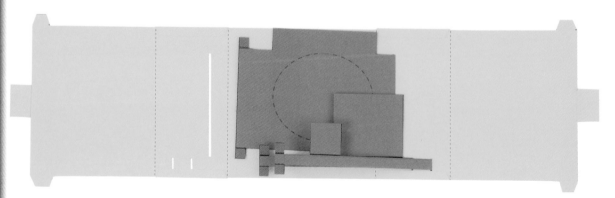

9 Glue the lower tabs of the mechanism holders in place on the wrong side of the stage front.

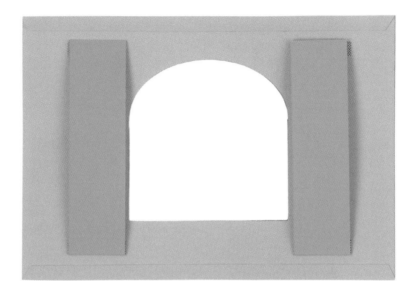

10 Insert the mechanism and glue the top tabs in place.

11 Glue the backing card to the centre panel.

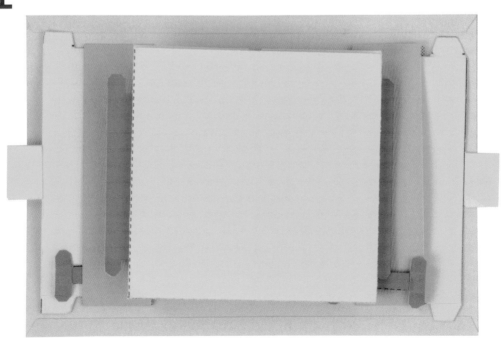

PULL-TAB SCROLL

The basic pull-tab can be easily adapted to create a variety of effects. The mechanism template was taken from a Victorian card in which a scroll is opened with a pull-tab and the example shows the mechanism reversed with additional images.

1 Remove the slot from the card. Glue a ⅜in (1cm) strip to the marked area for the pull-tab sleeve.

2 On the pull-tab, pierce a hole either end of the dotted line and reverse the card. Score between the pierced holes then fold and crease.

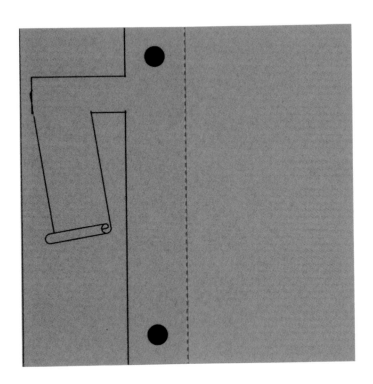

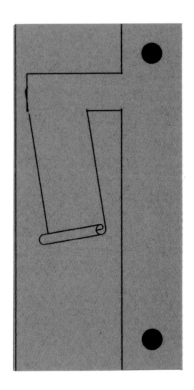

MATERIALS

- **Templates on page 140** transferred on to card
- Scissors
- Pin (to pierce holes)
- Bone folder
- Glue
- Strip of paper
- Strip of card

3 Glue together and cut along the solid lines. Punch holes where marked. Thread ribbon through the holes, leaving a length at either end, and secure on the back of the pull-tab with glue.

4 Insert the scroll through the slot in the card.

5 On the reverse side fold the tab sleeve over the tab.

6 With the scroll in its closed position, glue a narrow strip of card across the pull tab immediately below the sleeve.

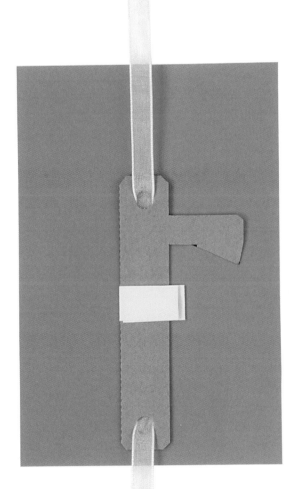

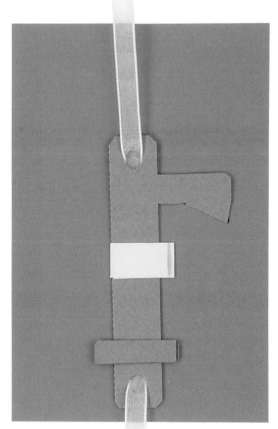

PULL-TAB BUTTERFLY WINGS

Operated by a pull-tab the upper sections of this design are lifted forward and outwards from the background to reveal a message or image hidden in the centre. The decorative oval has the dual function of concealing the mechanism and holding it in place, and should be cut sufficiently large enough for this purpose.

1 Score the dotted lines, cut out the wings and remove the small shaded areas.

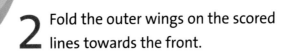

2 Fold the outer wings on the scored lines towards the front.

3 Fold the wings on the vertical scored lines towards the back.

MATERIALS

- **Templates on pages 141–142** transferred on to card
- Scissors
- Bone folder
- Glue
- Pin (to pierce holes)
- Wire
- Masking tape

4 Cut out the background card, remove the slots and glue the wing tab in the marked position.

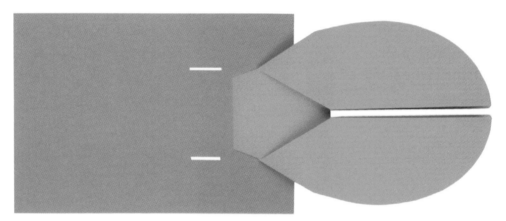

5 Score the long pull-tab, fold and glue. Pierce through both layers of card where marked. Score, fold and glue the small pull-tabs. Pierce the holes and fold back the ends on the scored lines. Join the three tabs with wire.

6 Pull the short pull-tabs through the slots in the background card, allowing ⅜in (1cm) to protrude from the top of the card.

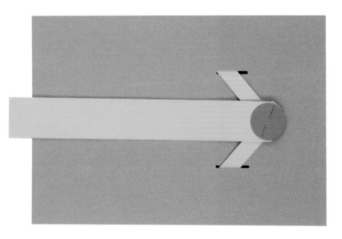

7 Hold in place with masking tape. Make a guide for the pull-tab and glue to the back of the card.

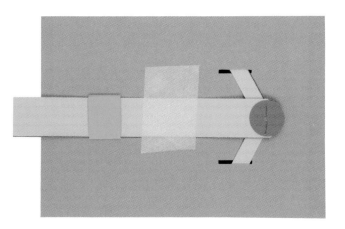

8 Apply glue spots to the centre of the folded back tabs. Bring up the wings and glue to the tabs.

9 Cut out the oval. Holding the tab in place with masking tape check the oval covers the cut edges of the wings and the wings open when the tab is pulled. Adjust the oval's position if necessary before gluing.

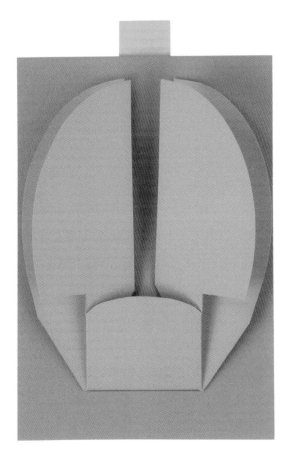

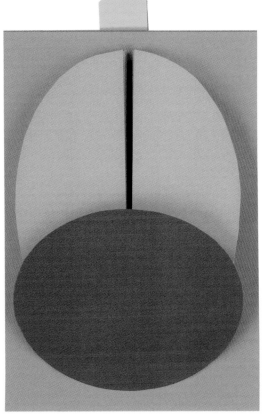

PULL-TAB FLOWER BOUQUET

This pull-tab design enables flowers or branches to extend outwards from the background, revealing hidden pictures or messages. The templates provided on page 143 are for a flower bouquet or a Christmas tree. They indicate the approximate sizes for the mechanism to slide smoothly. For the bouquet cut the seven templates roughly the same size. The three wider templates are for the centre of the Christmas tree. The Christmas tree was a popular design for cards, many of which were mechanical and operated by a pull-tab allowing the branches to part portraying flags, presents or simple greetings.

1 Remove the slots from the front of the card.

2 Score the dotted lines on A and cut out. Pierce the holes indicated below.

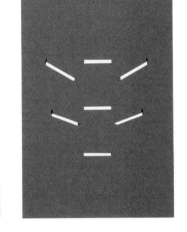

3 Score the dotted line on B/C, fold and pierce through both layers of card.

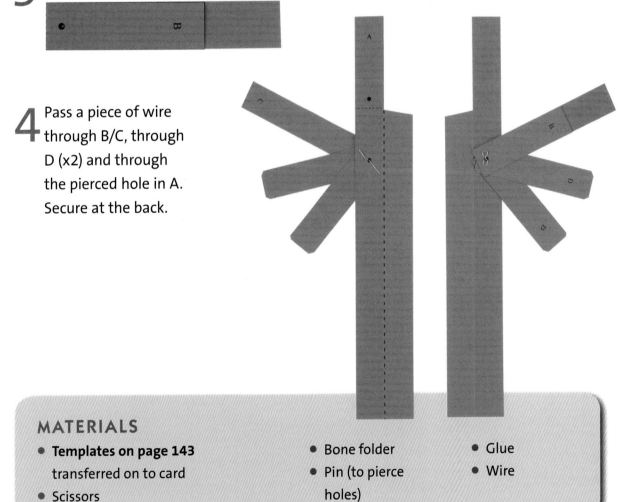

4 Pass a piece of wire through B/C, through D (x2) and through the pierced hole in A. Secure at the back.

MATERIALS

- **Templates on page 143** transferred on to card
- Scissors
- Bone folder
- Pin (to pierce holes)
- Glue
- Wire

PULL-TAB FLOWER BOUQUET

5 Fold on the scored line and glue.

6 Fold A on the scored line and pierce through all layers of card.

7 Thread wire through both the lower holes in A and E (x2). Secure at the back.

8 Slide the mechanism through the slots in the card and glue a slide holder on the back, as shown.

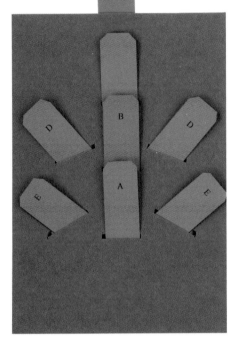

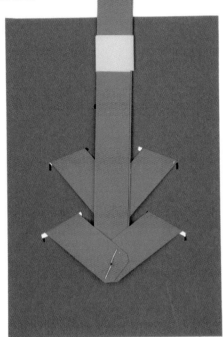

9 Finally, glue the decoration to the tabs on the front.

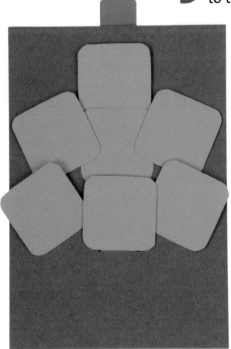

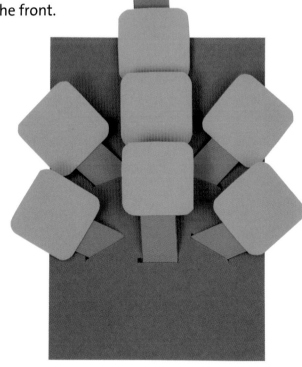

PULL-TAB FAN

Fans were a popular form of Valentine card and early examples show an abundance of floral designs. Valentine cards were frequently used for Christmas cards with the greetings appropriately altered.

1 Pierce holes where marked on the fan segments and cut out. *Note:* The upper hole in one segment is used as a guide line for gluing the thread and is not pierced.

2 Pierce the hole on the pull-tab, fold the scored area and cut out.

3 Fasten the fan segments together with wire, commencing with the segment with the unpierced hole.

4 Pass the wire through the hole in the pull-tab and bend back the ends.

MATERIALS
- **Templates on page 144** transferred on to card
- Scissors
- Pin (to pierce holes)
- Bone folder
- Wire
- Sewing needle
- Thread
- Masking tape
- Glue

5 Fold the pull-tab on the scored line and glue.

6 Fasten a long length of thread to the first segment and secure through the holes.

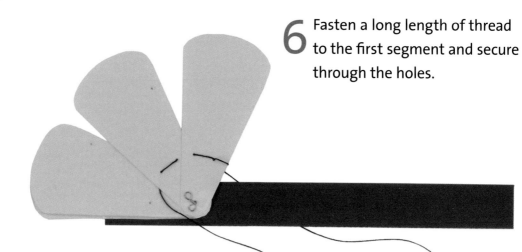

7 Bring the thread up and down through the two holes in the next segment.

8 Bring the two segments close together, slightly overlapping, and draw up the thread. Continue to thread the remaining segments, bringing the thread up and down through the two holes and overlapping the segments.

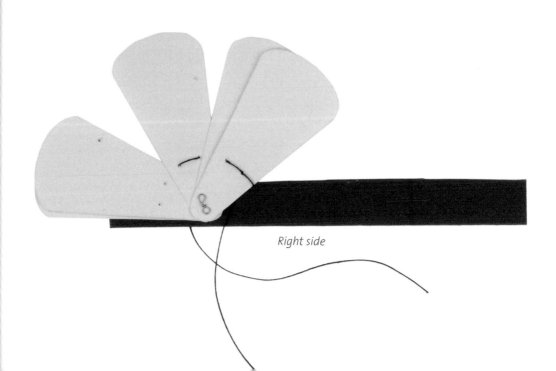

Right side

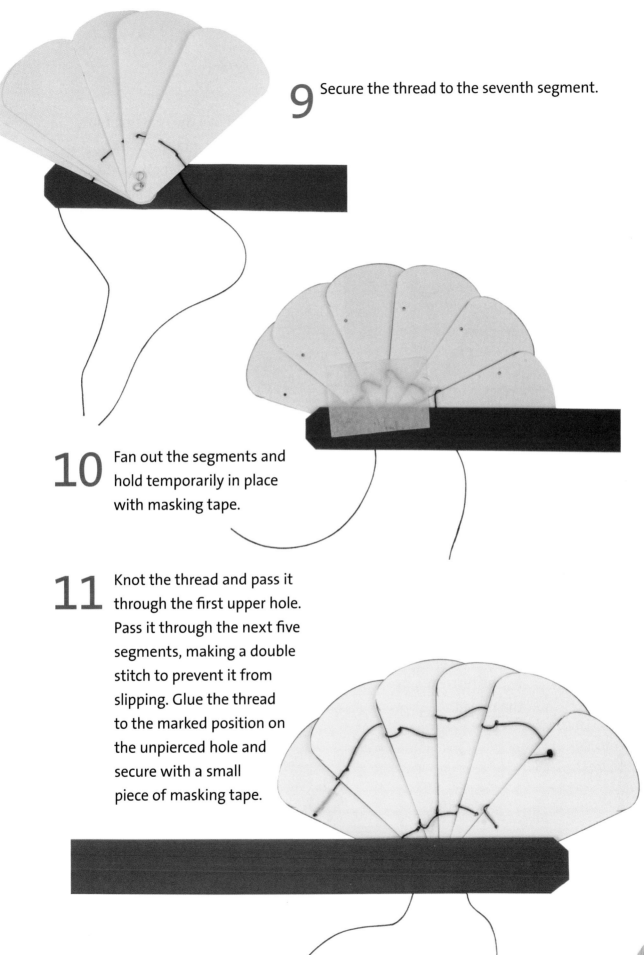

9 Secure the thread to the seventh segment.

10 Fan out the segments and hold temporarily in place with masking tape.

11 Knot the thread and pass it through the first upper hole. Pass it through the next five segments, making a double stitch to prevent it from slipping. Glue the thread to the marked position on the unpierced hole and secure with a small piece of masking tape.

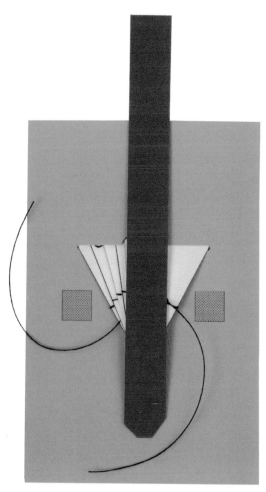

12 Remove the masking tape, close the fan, and with the longer length of the pull-tab facing upwards, push the segments through the slot in the backing card.

13 Open out the fan and pull the ends of the threads outwards from the slot. The open fan will be restricted by the thread.

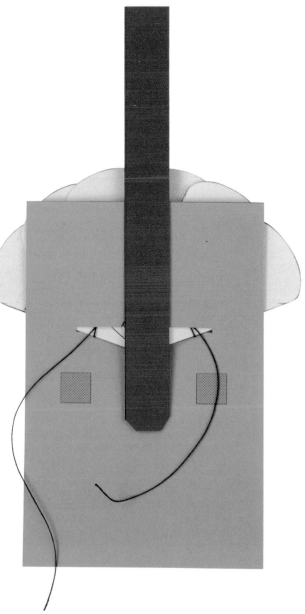

14 Bring the ends of the thread down to the marked positions on the backing card. Glue to the card and secure with masking tape. Cut away the excess thread. Make a slide for the pull-tab and glue to the backing card.

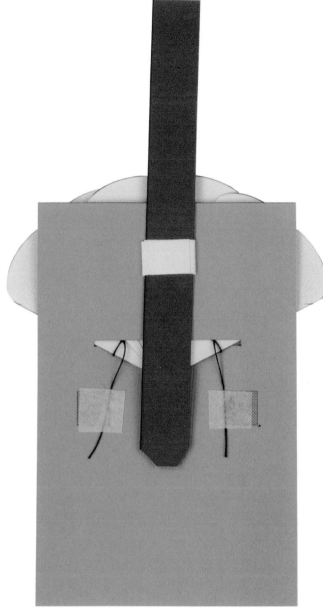

15 Glue a picture to the front of the card to conceal the fan.

PULL-TAB REVERSE

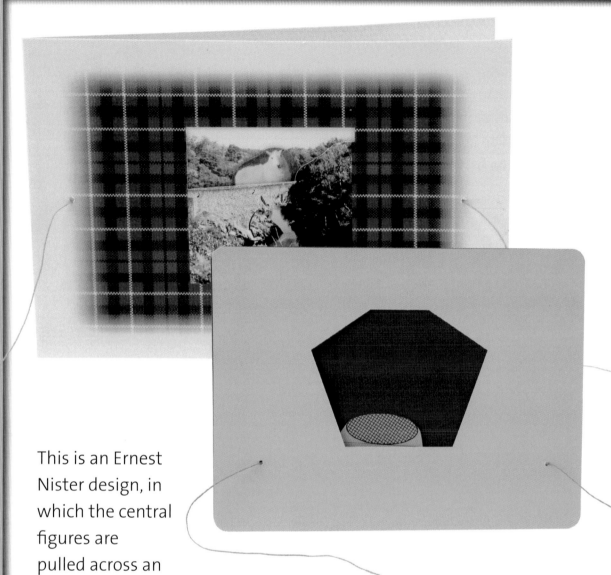

This is an Ernest Nister design, in which the central figures are pulled across an aperture in the card and 'magically' change direction. This device was used in Nister's pop-up *Come and Go* books. The advantage of the mechanism is that a car, train, sledge or similar will always travel forward, as opposed to other mechanisms where the vehicle must be pulled backwards to return it to the starting position. To achieve maximum effect, ensure that the thread is completely pulled across from one side to the other and then switch hands to allow the mechanism to pivot before pulling the thread in the opposite direction.

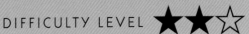
1 Remove the slot from the card back.

2 Remove the aperture from the card front and punch holes where indicated.

3 Pierce the holes in the mechanism. Thread a long length of thread through the two outer holes twice, glue the centre of the thread to the back of the card and for extra security cover with a piece of masking tape. *Note:* The shaded ovals on the mechanism indicate the position of the vehicle/figures and the lines above and below the central hole are the 'ground' level.

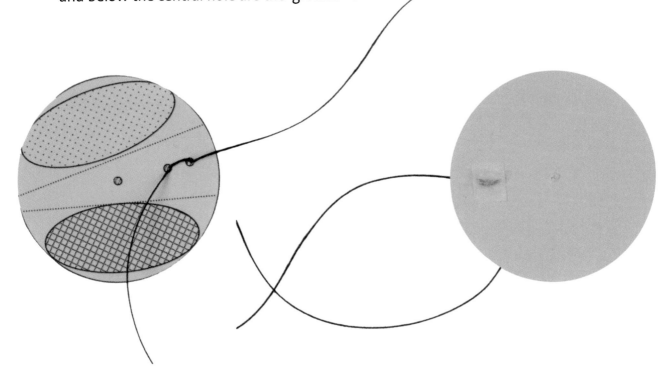

MATERIALS

- **Templates on pages 145–146** transferred on to card
- Scissors
- Hole punch
- Pin (to pierce holes)
- Thread
- Glue
- Masking tape
- Card
- Mini paper fastener

PULL-TAB REVERSE

4 Fasten the mechanism through the slot and secure at the back with a circle of card. A mini paper fastener is recommended for this. *Note:* The mechanism must be fastened loosely through the slot to allow it to rotate freely. Ensure that the mechanism moves smoothly along the slot – depending on the thickness of card, it may be necessary to increase the width of the slot.

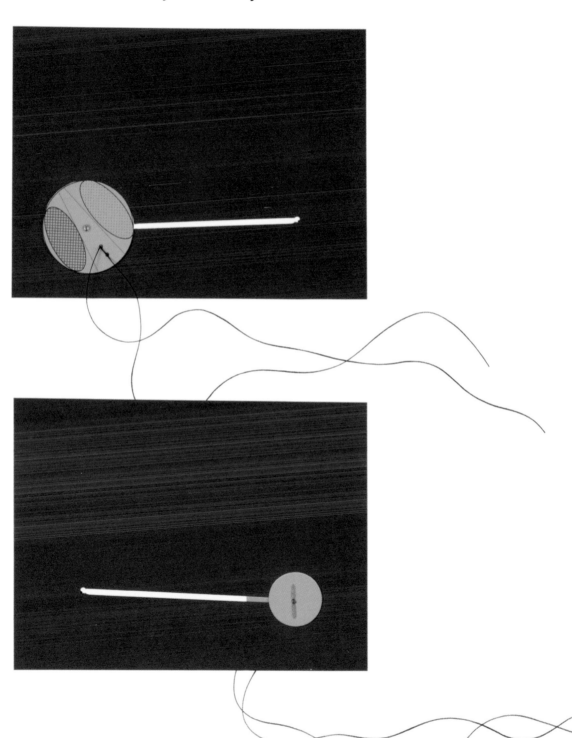

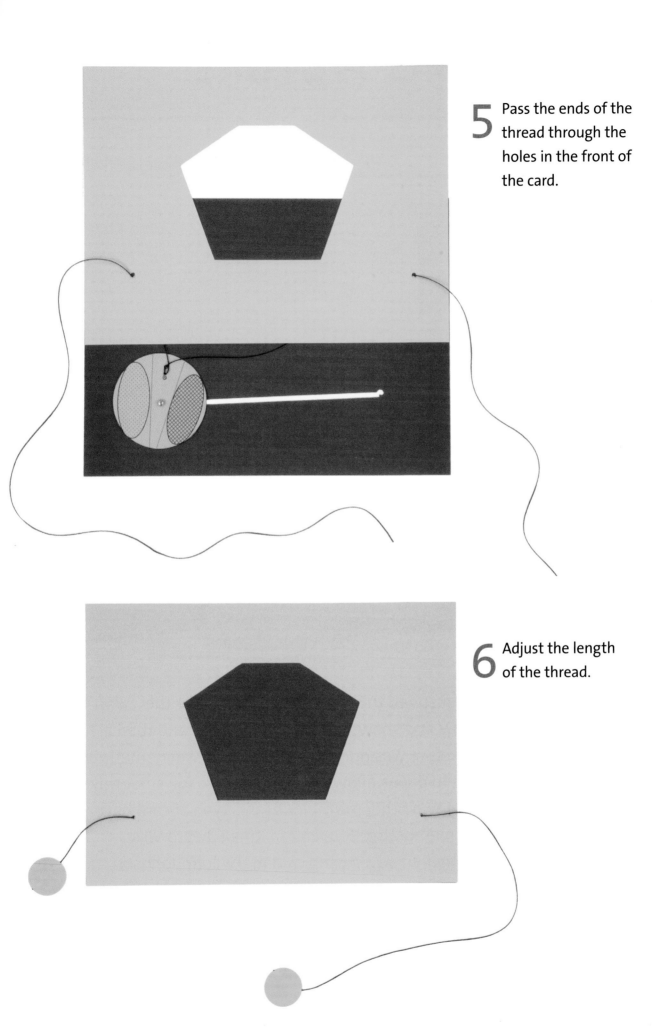

5 Pass the ends of the thread through the holes in the front of the card.

6 Adjust the length of the thread.

DISSOLVING PICTURE

The original card that inspired this design was printed for the Coronation of Edward V and shows him first as a prince and then as King. The dissolving picture was printed on silk, which was sometimes used as an alternative to paper, allowing the picture to roll smoothly through a buckle. Only two other examples of this type of card have been seen, one a commemorative souvenir of King Edward VII's Coronation and the other an advertising card in the John Johnson collection. The card mechanism functions smoothly without a buckle and this has been omitted from the template.

1 Score the dotted lines on the card front, fold and crease before removing the aperture and cutting out the card.

2 Score the centre of the pull-tab, fold, crease, cut out and glue.

3 Cut out the pictures.

4 Glue the pictures to either side of the aperture and fold back towards the ends of the card.

MATERIALS
- **Templates on pages 147–148** transferred on to card
- Bone folder
- Scissors
- Glue

5 Fold each picture across the aperture and crease the tabs towards the aperture.

6 Bring the left picture across the aperture and fold back the tab. Fold the right picture towards the end of the card.

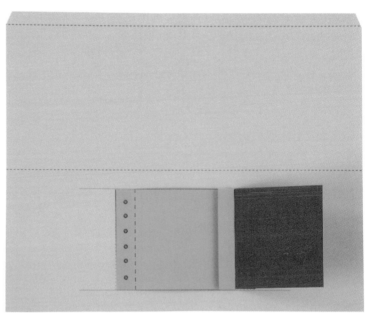

7 Glue the pull-tab to the picture tabs.

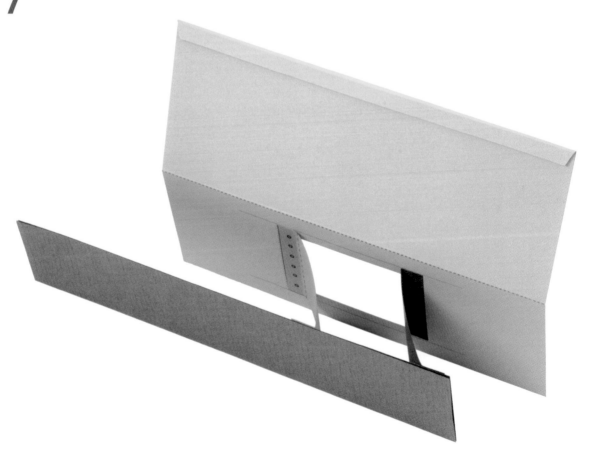

8 Glue along the edge of the card to enclose the mechanism.

DIAGONAL DISSOLVING

This mechanism was used by Ernest Nister in his book *What a Surprise*. It opens diagonally when the tab is pulled to reveal a different picture. Although the original mechanism appeared in a square frame, any aperture shape can be cut and a shell surround has been used for the example.

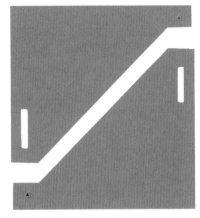

1 Take the moving picture template. Remove the slots, pierce the holes marked and round off the corners.

2 Now pierce the marked holes in the stationary picture backing.

3 Pierce a hole in the pull-tab where marked, then score, fold and glue. Repierce the hole through the folded and glued card.

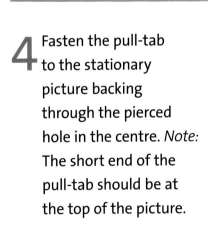

4 Fasten the pull-tab to the stationary picture backing through the pierced hole in the centre. *Note: The short end of the pull-tab should be at the top of the picture.*

MATERIALS
- **Templates on pages 149–150** transferred on to card
- Scissors
- Pin (to pierce holes)
- Glue
- Masking tape

DIAGONAL DISSOLVING

5 Push the ends through a circle of card on the back.

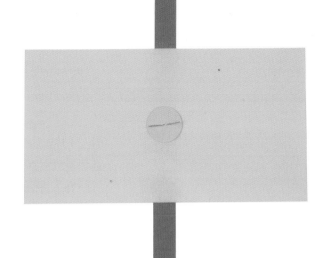

6 Glue the short edges of the stationary picture to the backing card where marked.

7 With the right side of the moving picture facing you, slide the slots over the pull-tab and fasten wire through the pierced corners to the backing card. Bend over the ends and secure with a circle of card and small pieces of masking tape. The mechanism is now complete.

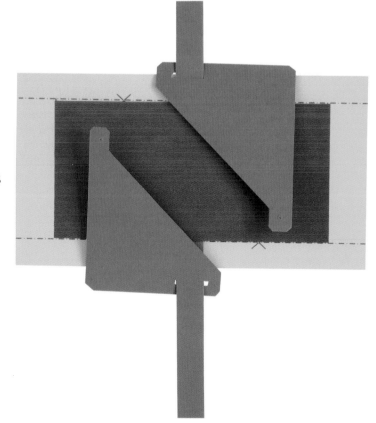

8 Cut out the front of the card. Remove the central aperture and cut a slit for the pull-tab.

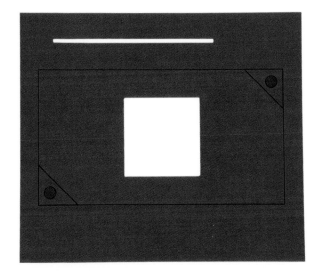

9 Push the tab through the slit and line up the mechanism in the marked position on the back of the aperture. Hold the corners in place with masking tape. Turn to the right side and check that the picture is correctly aligned to the aperture. Glue the mechanism to the back of the aperture with glue spots where marked.

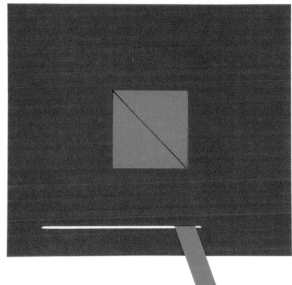

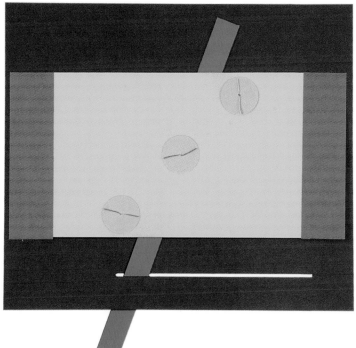

FLY-AWAY DISSOLVING

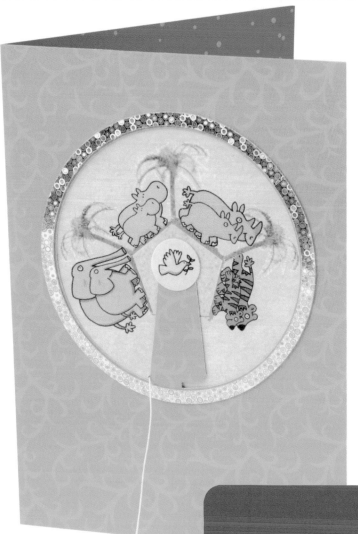

Dean and Nister both included these mechanisms in their children's pop-up books and adapted the design for cards. In this early dissolving picture a large part of the design is covered with the stand, thereby concealing the mechanism.

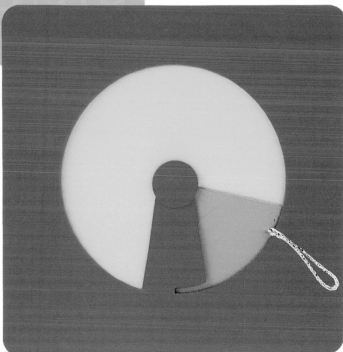

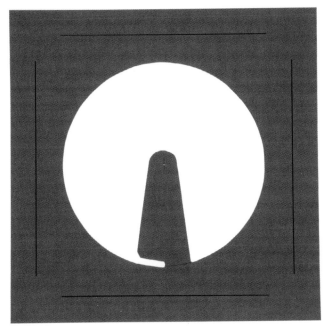

1 Cut out the aperture from the card front.

2 Cut out the circle from the moving disk or just remove the corners. Pierce a large hole where marked and pass the ends of a folded piece of thick thread through the hole. Glue the ends to the wrong side and secure with masking tape. Cut from the centre to the lower edge.

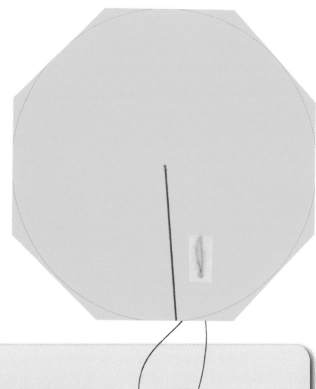

MATERIALS

- **Templates on pages 151–152** transferred on to card
- Scissors
- Pin (to pierce holes)
- Thick thread
- Masking tape
- Glue
- Wire
- Card

FLY-AWAY DISSOLVING

3 Cut the solid line from the centre to the lower edge of the stationary disk.

4 With right sides facing upwards, interlock the moving disk and the stationary disk through the cut slots, matching up the centres. Pierce a larger hole through the centre with a pin. Ensure that the thread hangs freely at the front of the card.

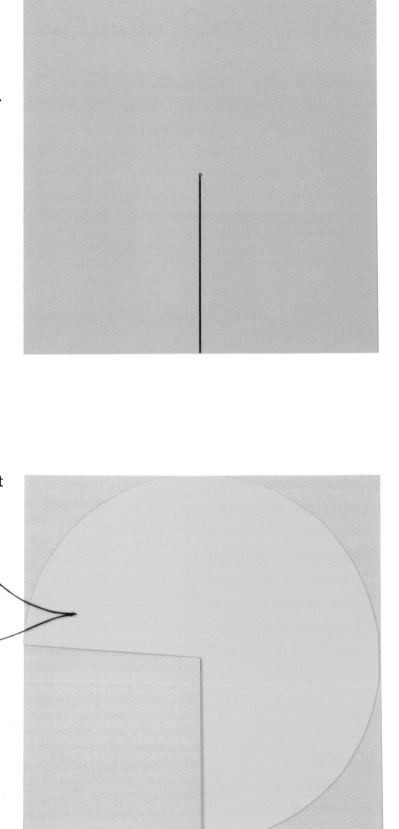

5 Align the square stationary disk with the marked lines on the back of the aperture and temporarily hold in place at the corners with masking tape. Pass a piece of wire through the centre of the aperture, disks and a small circle of waste card.

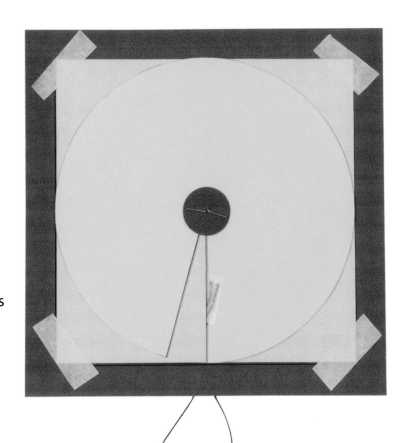

6 Apply glue to the corners of the stationary disk and press firmly to the card front.

7 On the right side cover the wire in the centre of the aperture with a card circle or shape.

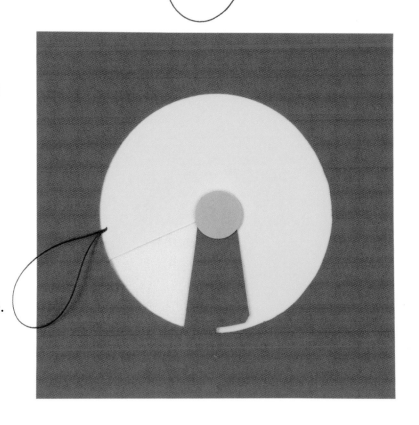

KALEIDOSCOPE DISSOLVING

This card is based on an Ernest Nister dissolving picture cut from six interlocked segments and operated by a pull-tab. The design was an improvement on the Flyaway Dissolving (see page 106), as the small central boss allowed more of the picture to be viewed.

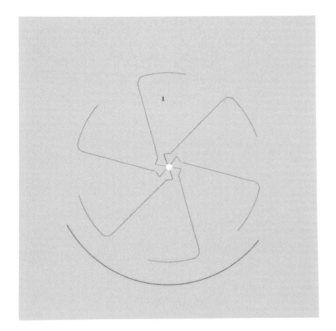

1 Take the stationary picture template. Cut along the solid lines and pierce a small hole in the centre.

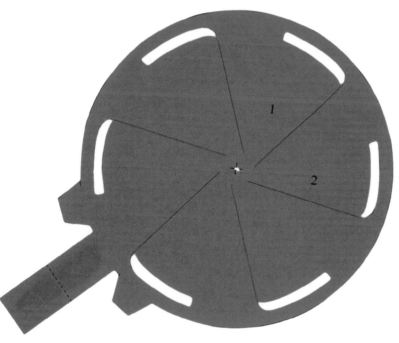

2 Take the moving picture template. Remove the slots and cut through the solid lines to the inner marked circle. Pierce a small hole in the centre. Score, fold and glue the pull-tab.

MATERIALS
- **Templates on pages 153–154** transferred on to card
- Scissors
- Pin (to pierce holes)
- Craft knife
- Card
- Wire

KALEIDOSCOPE DISSOLVING

3 Insert segment 1 of the stationary picture through segments 1 and 2 of the moving picture.

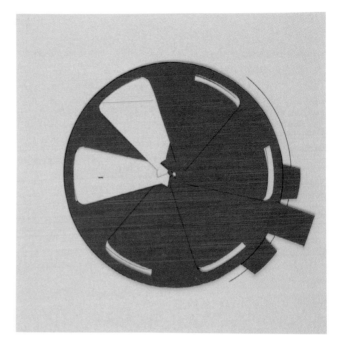

4 Thread the pull-tab through the slot and insert the remaining five segments through the moving disk to complete the interlocked pictures.

5 Cut two card circles large enough to cover the interlocking sections on the front. Loop a piece of wire and pass through one circle and the centre of the pictures.

6 On the wrong side pass the ends of the wire through the second card circle and bend the ends down to hold the pictures in place.

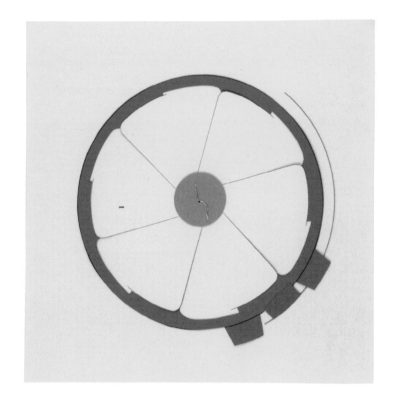

7 Cover the wire loop on the front with a card circle or punched shape.

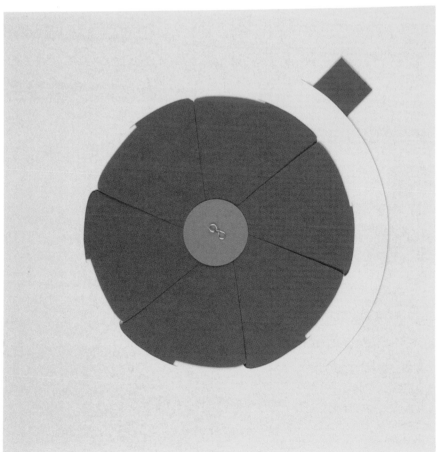

VENETIAN BLIND DISSOLVING

This is a dissolving picture cut
on the Venetian Blind principle.
It requires two identical pictures
for each scene.

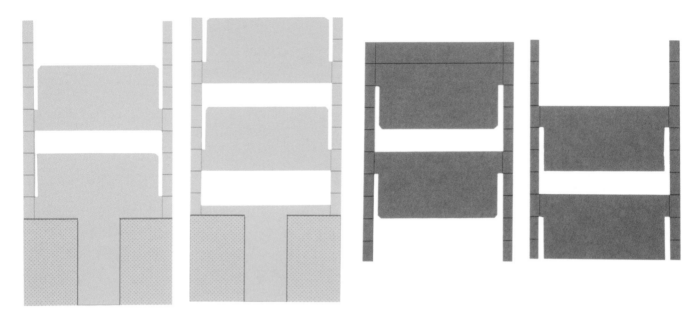

1 There are four parts to cut for the mechanism: two for the stationary picture and two for the moving picture. Remove the shaded areas but do not cut the pull-tab.

2 Fold a strip of paper round the stationary picture, crease along the edges and open out. Trim the edges to ³⁄₁₆in (0.5cm) wide.

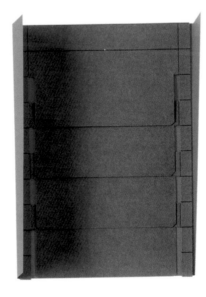
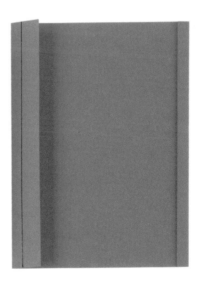

MATERIALS
- **Templates on pages 155–156** transferred on to card
- Scissors
- Glue
- Masking tape
- Strip of paper

3 Interlock the stationary picture segments and glue together down the long outside strips. Repeat with the moving picture segments, gluing together down the long outside strips and across the marked pull-tab. Remove the shaded areas either side of the pull-tab.

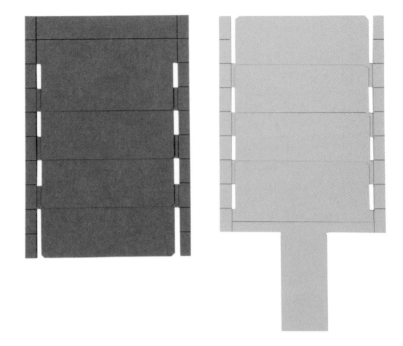

4 Interlock the stationary and moving pictures.

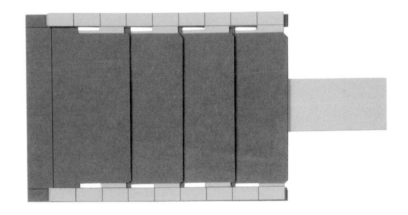

5 Place the mechanism behind the card aperture, thread the pull-tab through the slot, and align the top of the stationary picture along the dotted line. Hold the mechanism lightly in place with masking tape.

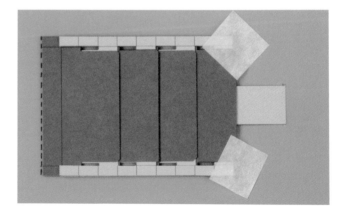

6 Glue a narrow strip of paper across the top of the stationary picture to secure it to the frame.

7 Fold the mechanism towards the top of the card. Wrap the paper strip round the mechanism and glue the edges to the sides of the stationary picture.

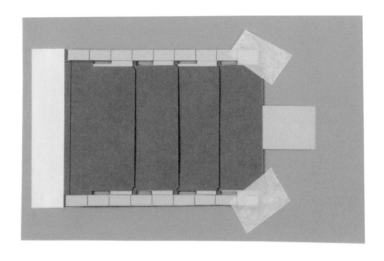

8 Apply spots of glue to the paper strip edges and fold down to secure the mechanism to the sides of the aperture, rethreading the pull-tab through the slot.

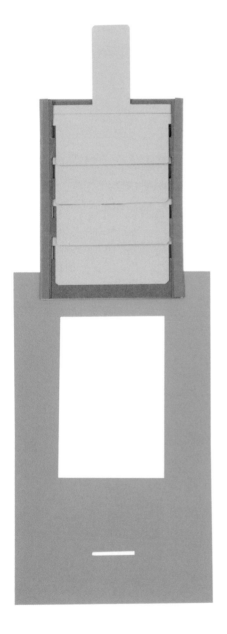

VENETIAN BLIND VARIATION

This sliding mechanism requires two contrasting pictures, and you can have fun decorating the background card, too. In the previous examples of dissolving pictures there was image loss to one or more pictures but the Venetian Blind mechanism allows each picture to remain complete.

1 Cut along all the solid black lines.

2 Take the stationary picture template and pin-prick through the corners of the dotted 'frame'. Remove the slot.

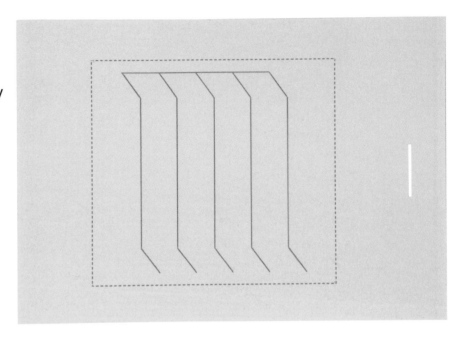

3 Take the moving picture. Score and fold the pull-tab forward then glue it together.

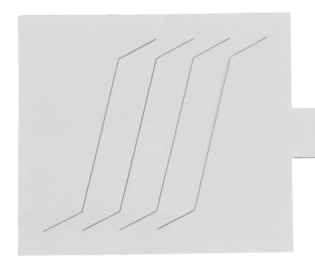

MATERIALS
- **Templates on pages 157–158** transferred onto card
- Scissors
- Pin (to pierce holes)
- Bone folder
- Glue

VENETIAN BLIND VARIATION

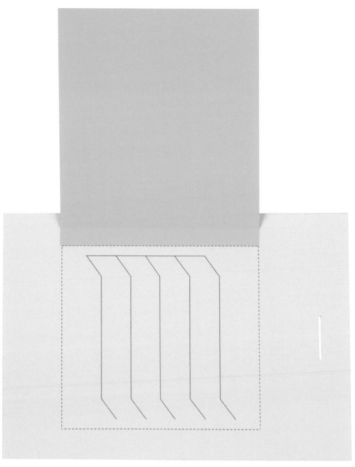

4 Glue the slide cover to the top of the stationary picture.

5 Insert the stationery picture strips through the slots in the moving picture. Thread the pull-tab through the slot in the stationary picture. Apply small spots of glue to the top of each cut strip in the stationary picture. Fold the slide cover down over the glue spots.

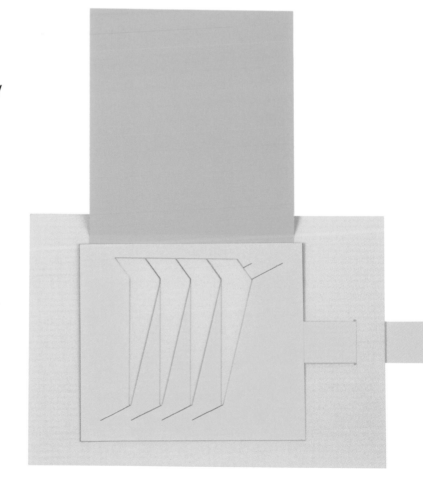

6 Fold up the bottom edge of the slide cover, allowing sufficient ease for the pull-tab to slide freely.

7 Refold and tuck under the lower edge of the moving picture.

8 Cut the frame, removing the centre. The pin pricks on the stationary picture mark the position of the frame. Apply glue to the corners of the frame and glue to the marked position on the stationary picture. Reduce the length of the pull-tab if required.

TEMPLATES

PUZZLE PURSE

PAPER SPRINGS

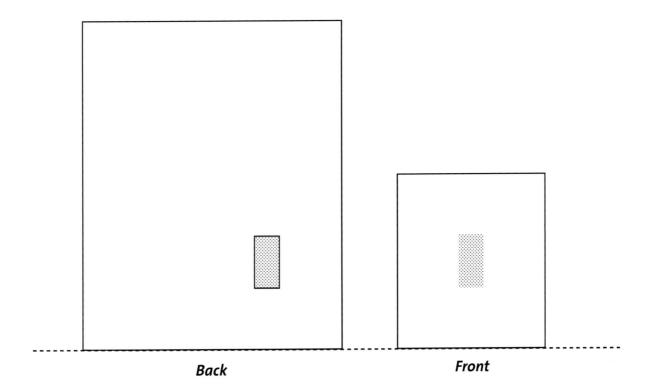

Back

Front

Paper Spring

PAPER CAGE

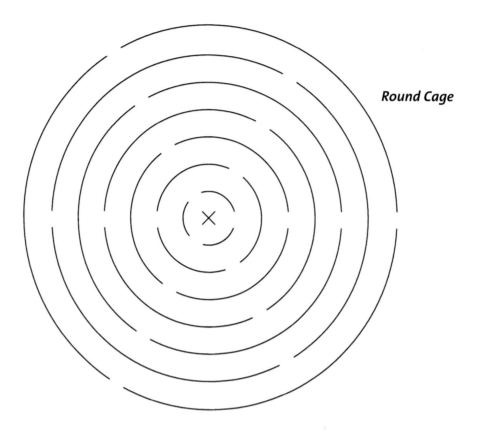

Round Cage

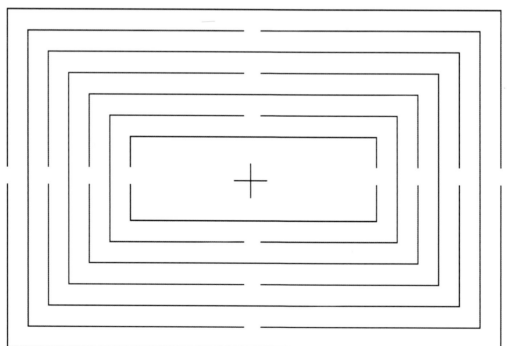

Rectangular Cage

ACCORDION
FOLD

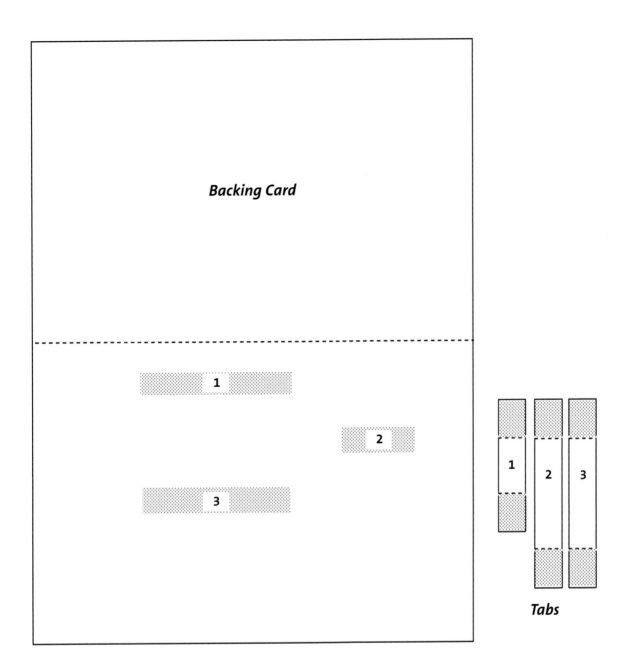

Backing Card

1

2

3

1

2

3

Tabs

90° BASIC CARD

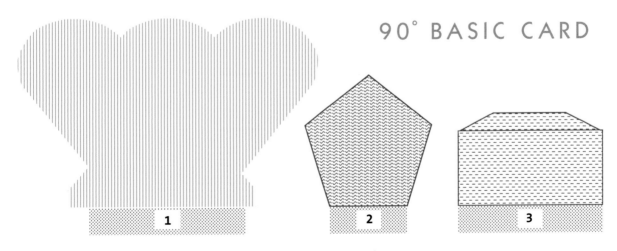

1

2

3

Figures/Scenery

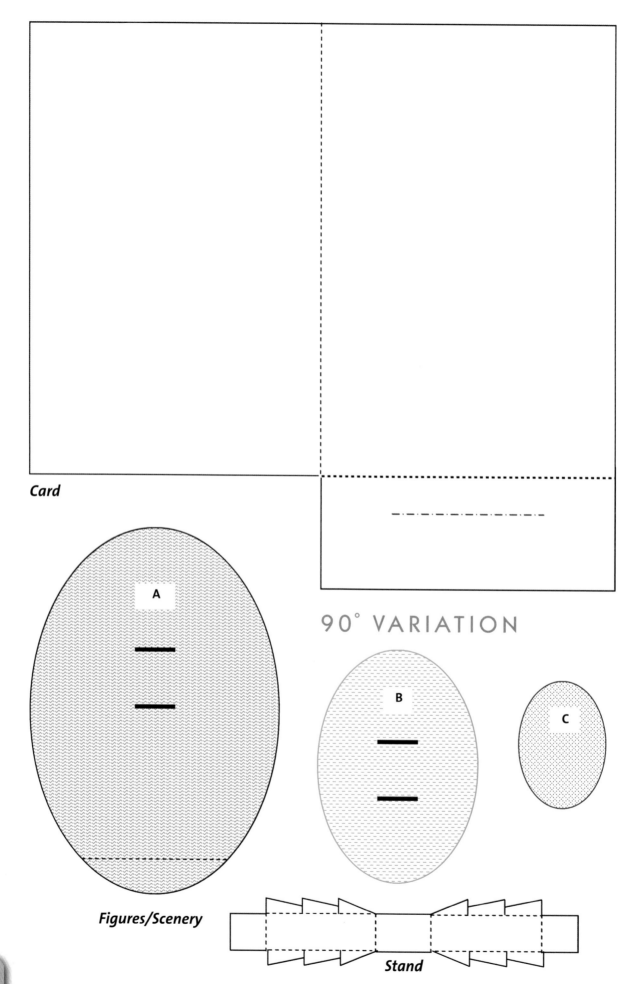

Card

90° VARIATION

A

B

C

Figures/Scenery

Stand

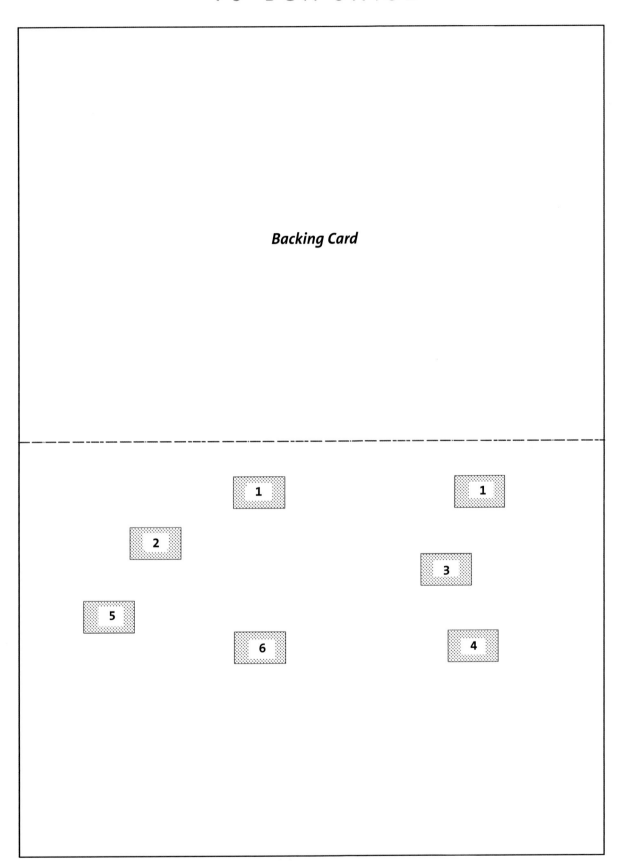

Backing Card

3	**6**	**2**

1	**1**

4

5

Figures/Scenery

90° BOX STAGE

Wrong Side

1   **1**

2

3

5

4   **6**

Stage

90° SLEEVE STAGE

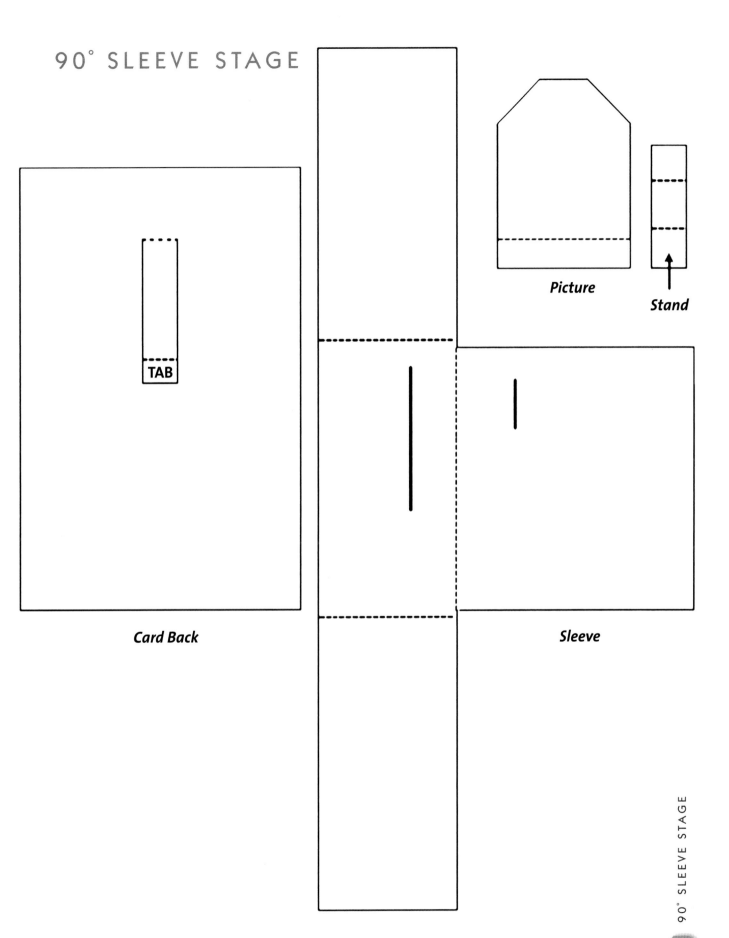

TAB

Card Back

Picture

Stand

Sleeve

90° WIDE PULL-TAB STAGE

Right Side
Picture on this side
Top of picture facing upwards

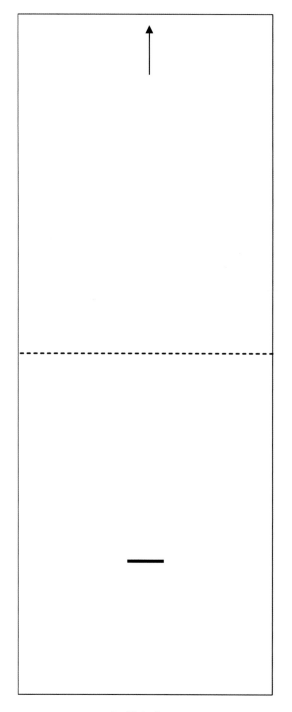

Pull-tab

Ribbon Slot

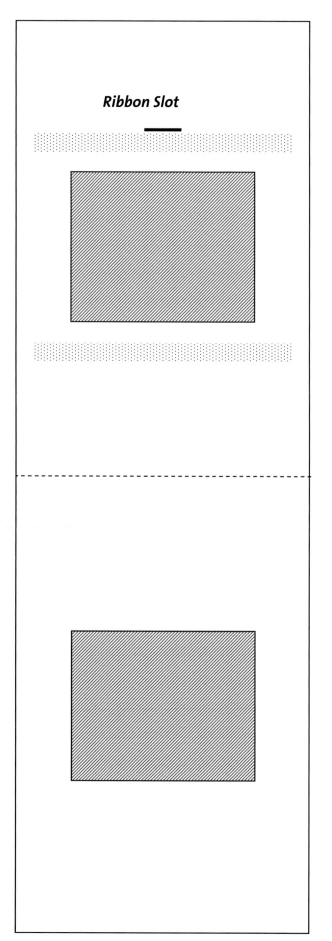

Card Front
Right side

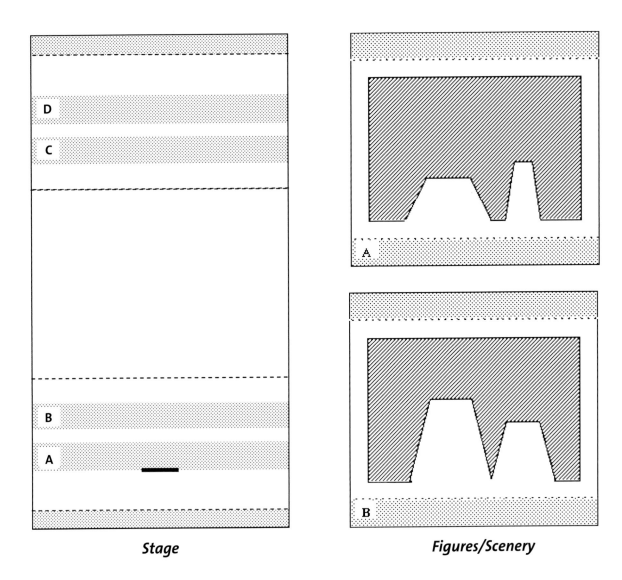

Stage

Figures/Scenery

90° WIDE PULL-TAB STAGE

Backing Card

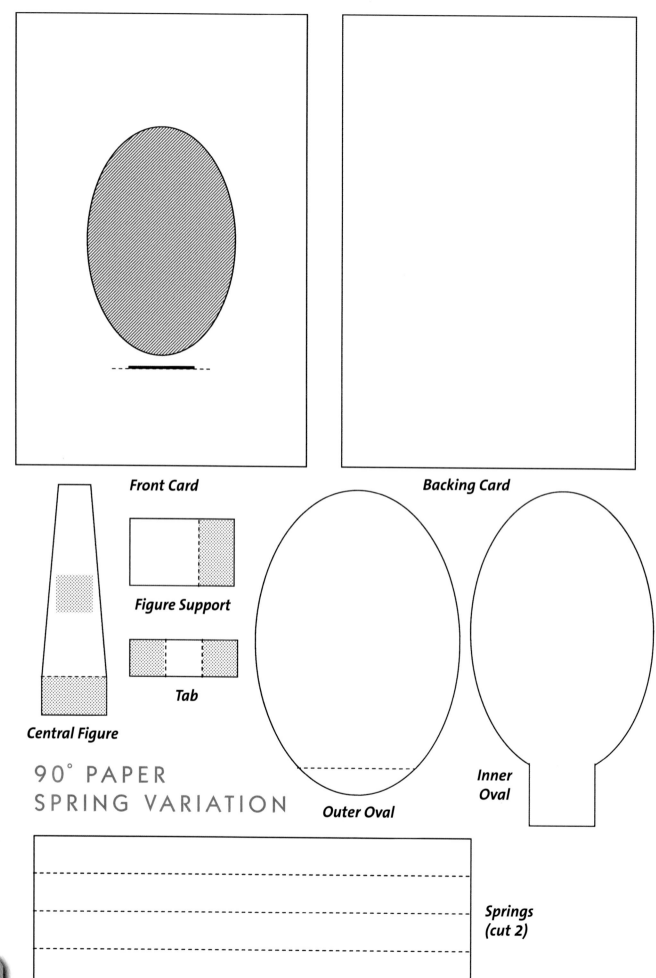

Front Card

Backing Card

Figure Support

Tab

Central Figure

Outer Oval

Inner Oval

90° PAPER SPRING VARIATION

Springs (cut 2)

Middle Layer

Top Layer

Backing Card

TAB

TAB

TAB

TAB

180° BASIC CARD

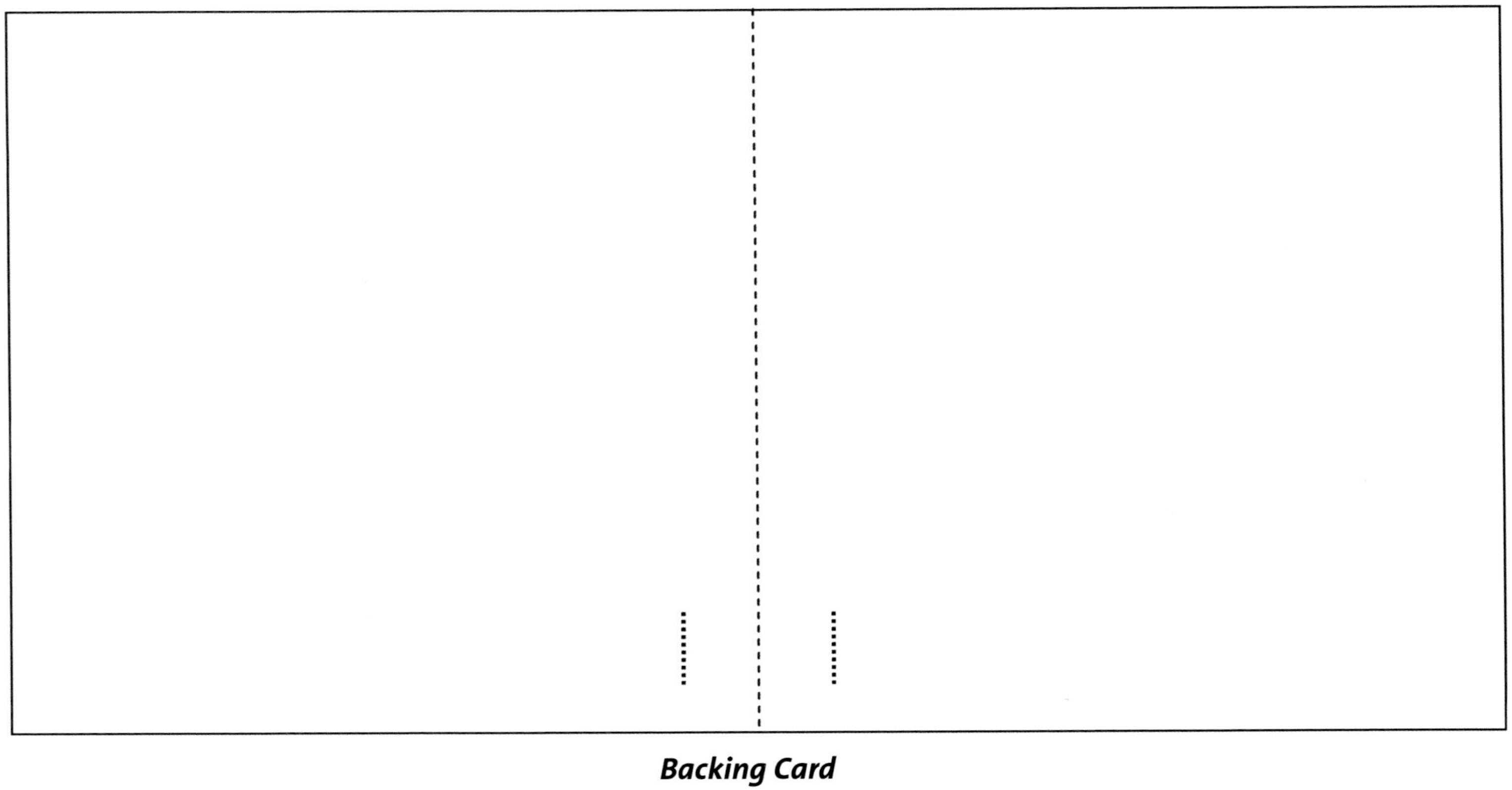

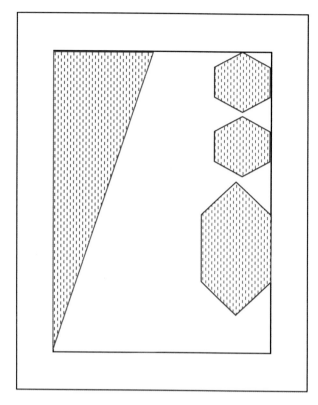

Scene One

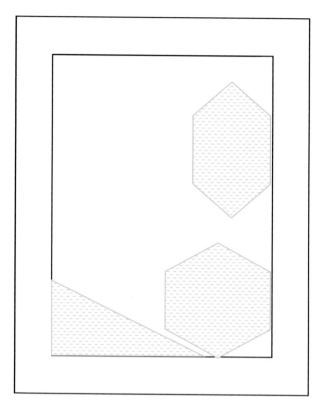

Scene Two

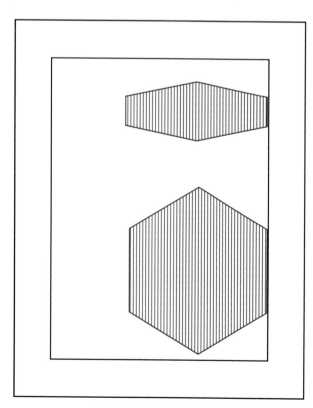

Scene Three

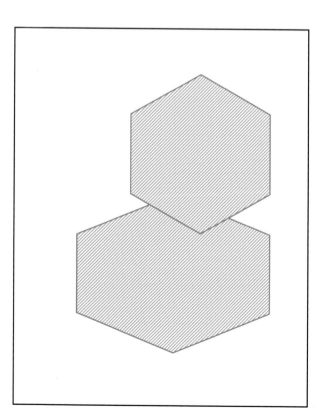

Background

180° PEEPSHOW

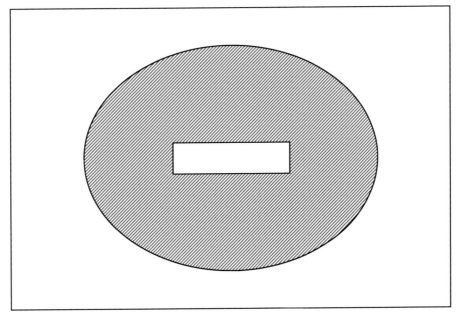

Front

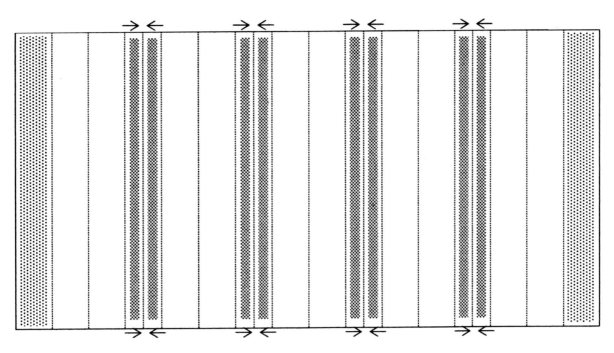

Paper Spring (cut 2)

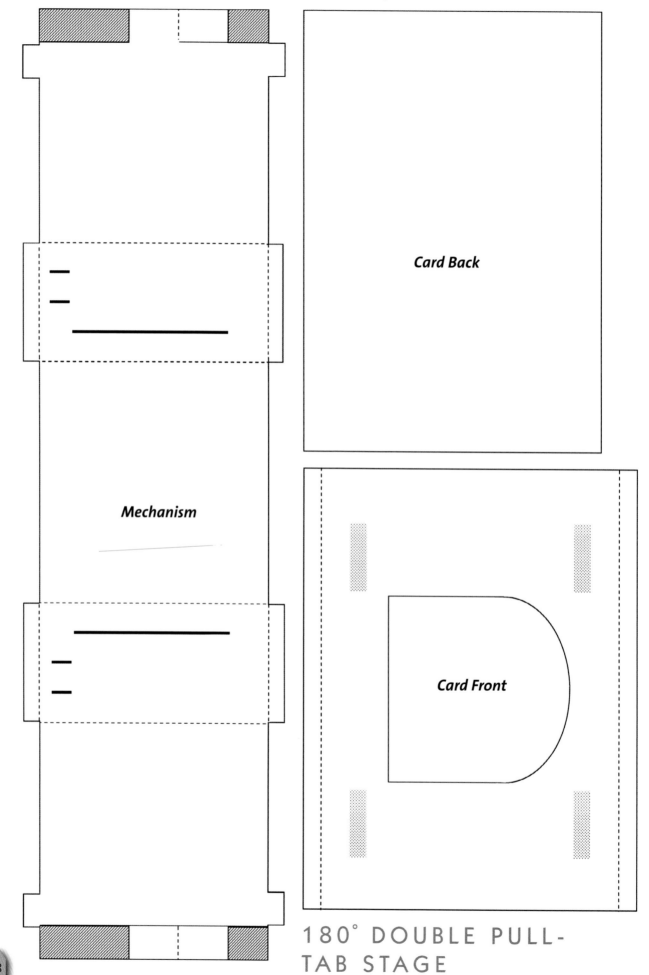

Card Back

Mechanism

Card Front

180° DOUBLE PULL-
TAB STAGE

180° DOUBLE PULL-TAB STAGE

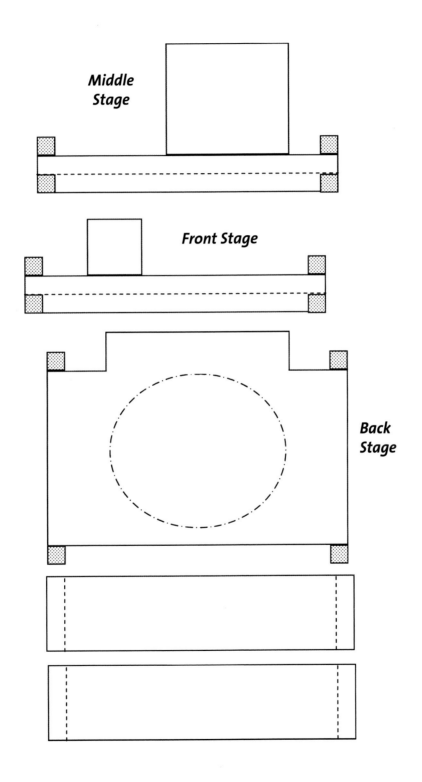

Middle Stage

Front Stage

Back Stage

PULL-TAB SCROLL

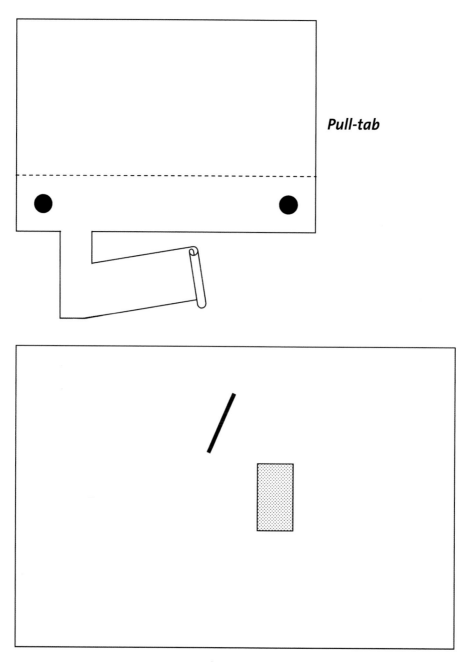

Pull-tab

Backing Card

PULL-TAB
BUTTERFLY
WINGS

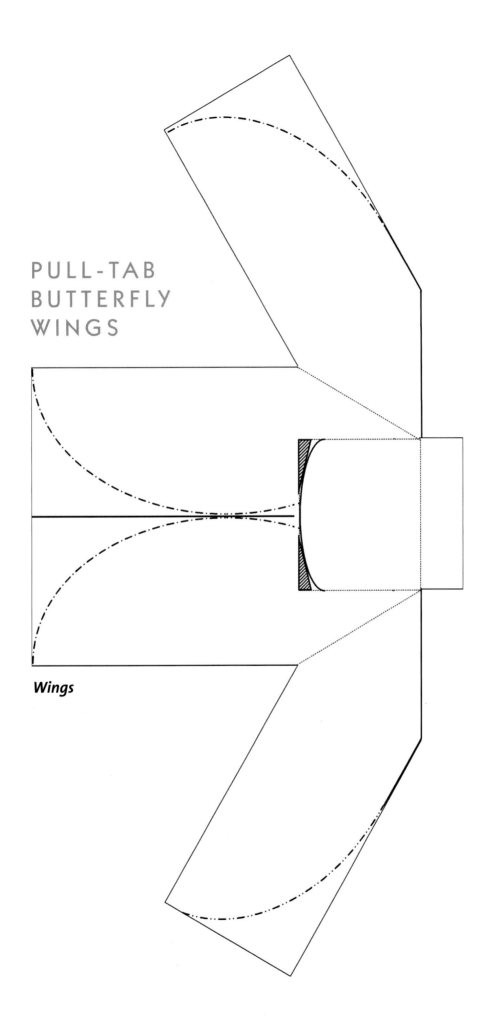

Wings

PULL-TAB BUTTERFLY WINGS

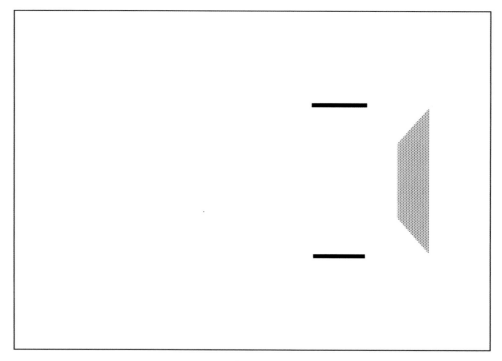

Backing Card

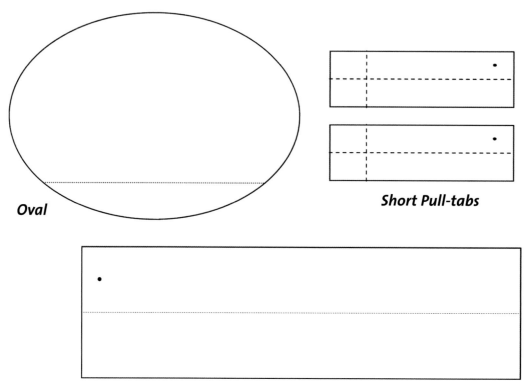

Oval

Short Pull-tabs

Long Pull-tab

A

D

D

E

E

B

C

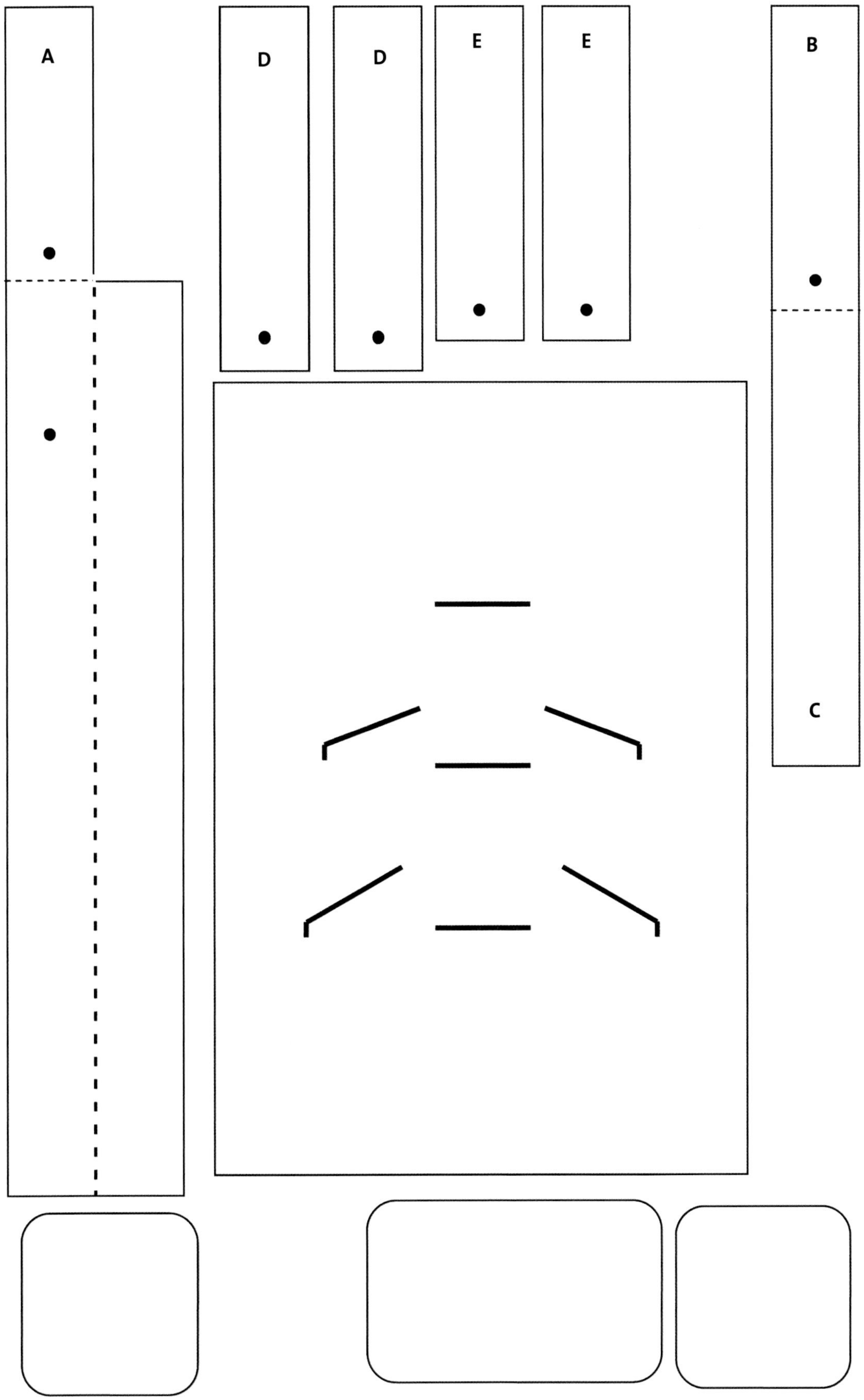

**Decoration Flowers
(cut 7)**

**Decoration Christmas
Tree Centre (cut 3)**

**Christmas Tree
(cut 4)**

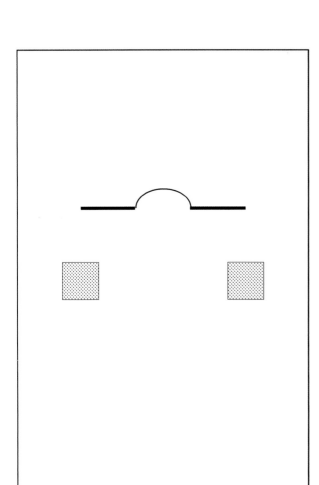

Backing Card

Front Picture

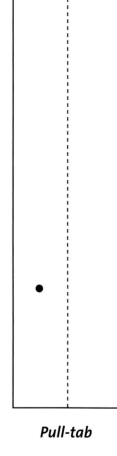

Pull-tab

PULL-TAB FAN

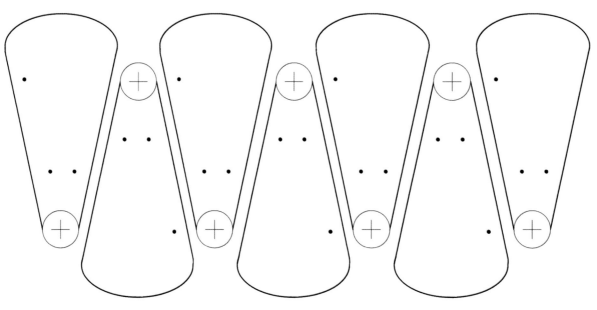

Fan Segments

PULL-TAB REVERSE

Card Front – Inside

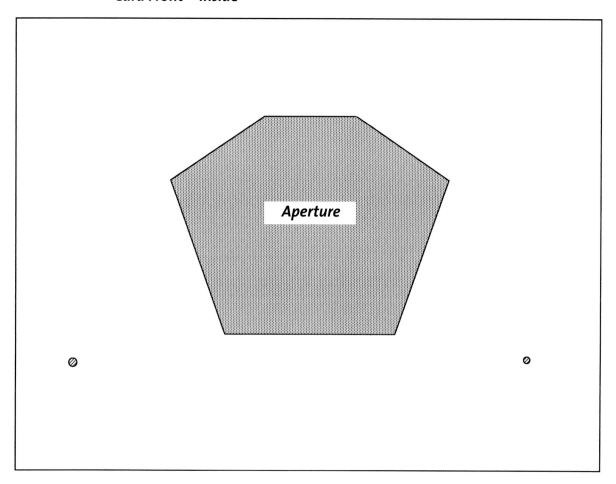

Aperture

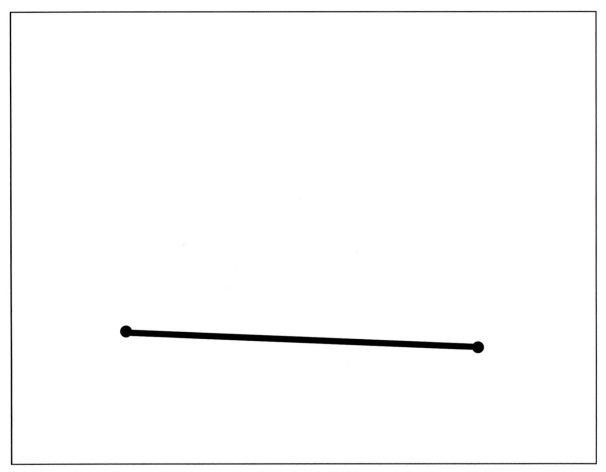

Card Back – Outside

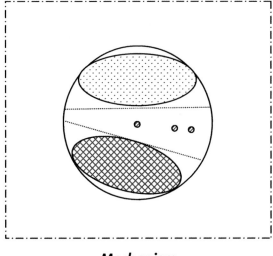

Mechanism

DISSOLVING PICTURE

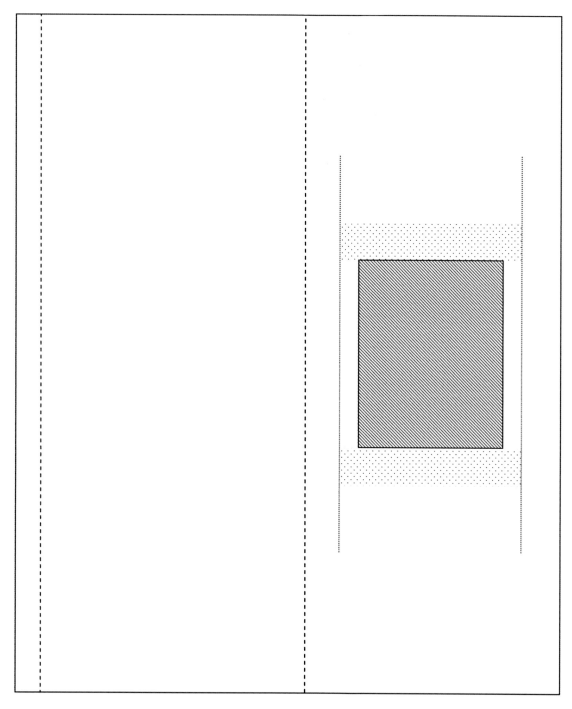

Card Front

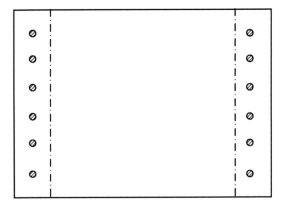

Picture 1

Picture 2

DISSOLVING
PICTURE

Pull-tab

DIAGONAL DISSOLVING

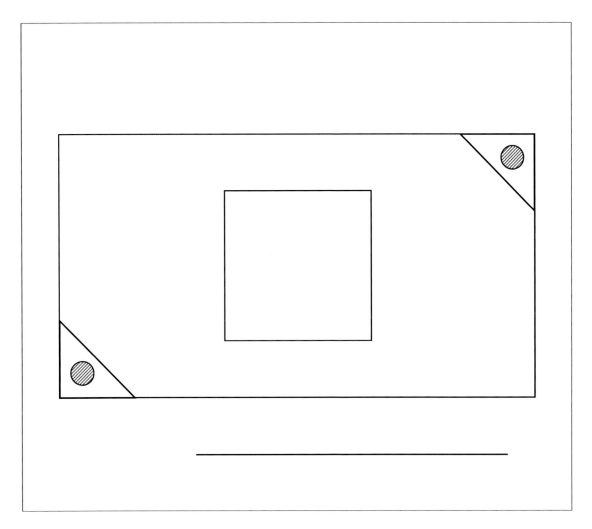

Card Front

DIAGONAL DISSOLVING

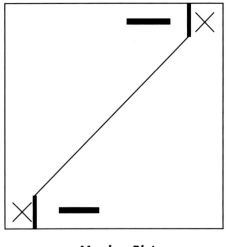

Moving Picture

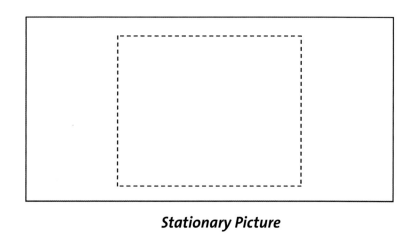

Stationary Picture

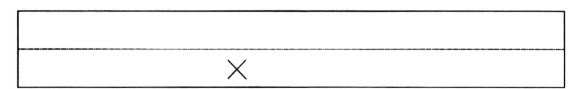

Pull-tab

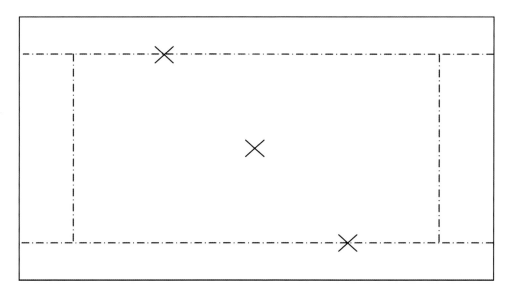

Stationary Picture Backing

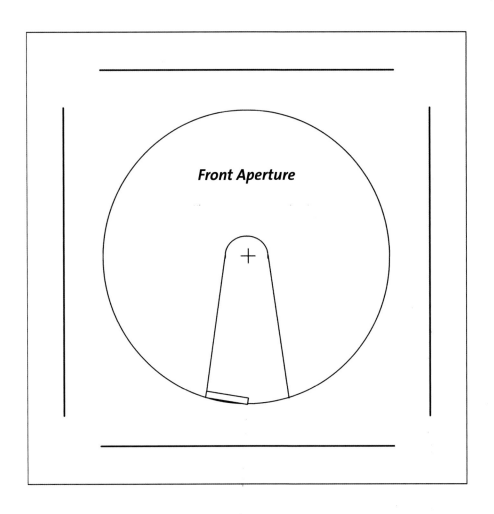

Front Aperture

FLY-AWAY DISSOLVING

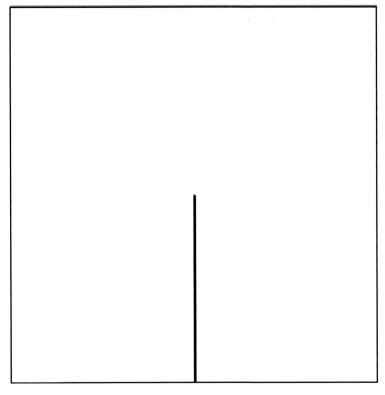

Stationary Disk

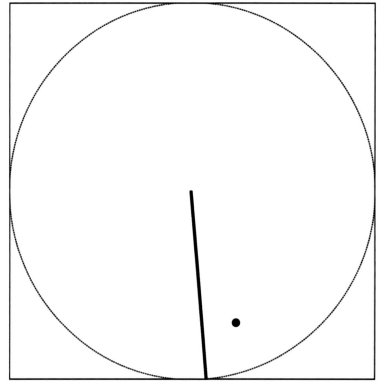

Moving Disk

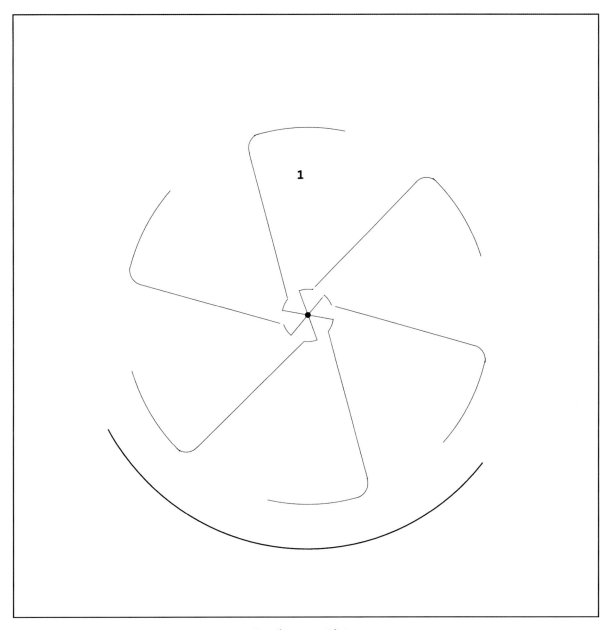

Stationary Picture

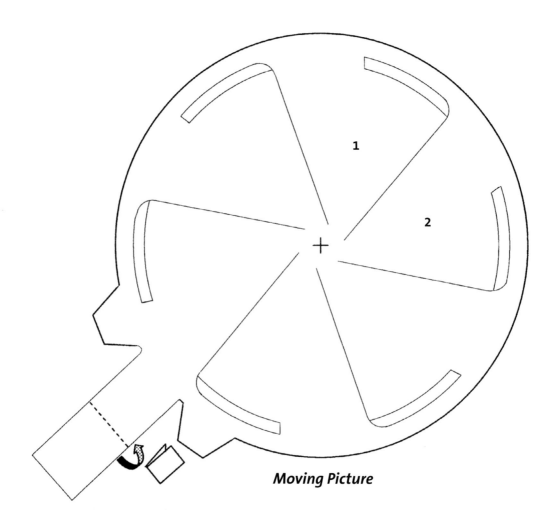

Moving Picture

VENETIAN BLIND DISSOLVING

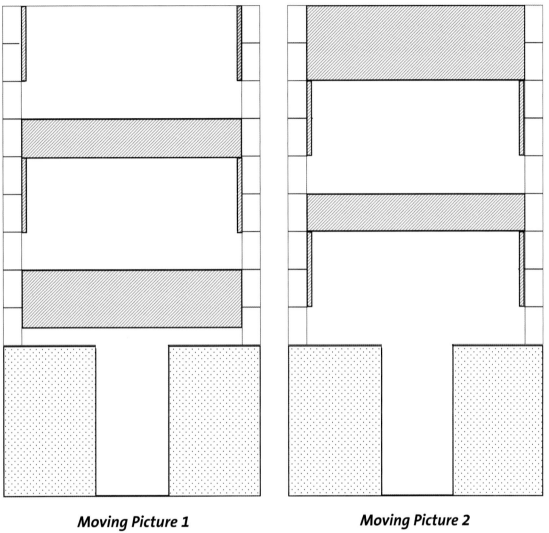

Moving Picture 1   **Moving Picture 2**

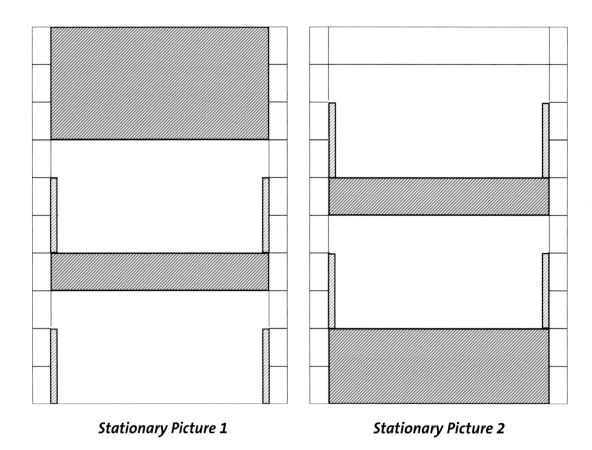

Stationary Picture 1　　　　　**Stationary Picture 2**

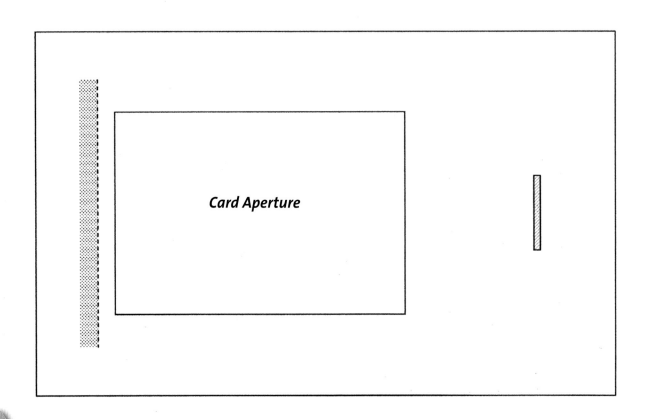

Card Aperture

VENETIAN BLIND VARIATION

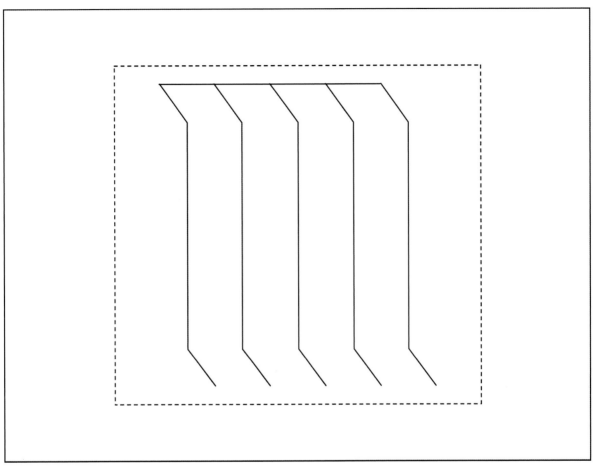

Stationary Picture

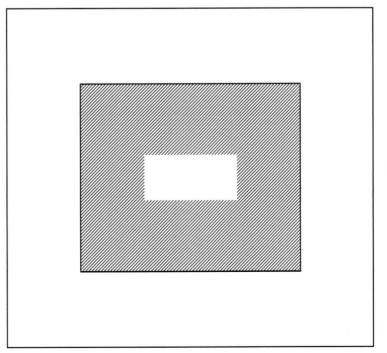

Picture Frame

VENETIAN BLIND VARIATION

Slide Cover *(Cut from paper)*

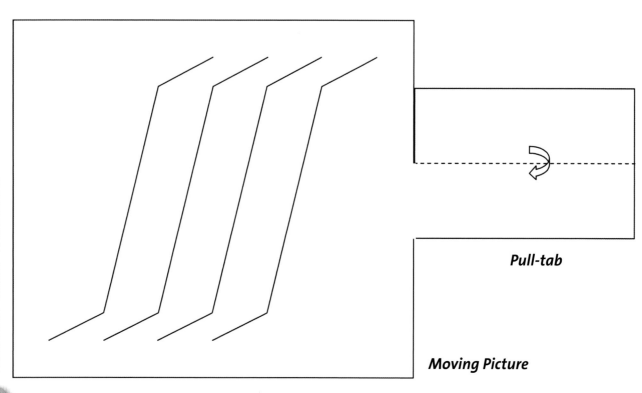

Pull-tab

Moving Picture

CARD COLLECTIONS IN THE UK

Laura Seddon Collection, Manchester Metropolitan University, All Saints, Manchester M15 6BH
Harry Page Collection, Manchester Metropolitan University, All Saints, Manchester M15 6BH
Queen Mary's Private Collection, British Museum, Great Russell Street, London WC1B 3DG
Jonathan King Valentine Collection, Museum of London, London Wall, London EC2Y 5HN
George Buday Collection, Victoria & Albert Museum Cromwell Road, London SW7 2RL
John Johnson Collection, Bodleian Library, Oxford University, Broad Street, Oxford OX1 3BG
York Castle Museum, Eye of York, York, YO1 9RY

CARD COLLECTIONS IN THE US

American Antiquarian Society, 185 Salisbury St., Worcester, MA 01609-508-755-5221
Cooper Hewitt National Design Museum, 2 E. 91st St., New York, NY 10128-212-860-6891
Hallmark Archives, Hallmark Cards-453, Box 419580, Kansas City, MO 64141
John Grossman Collection, The Gifted Line, 999 Canal Blvd., Pt. Richmond, CA 94804510-215-4777
New York Historical Society, 170 Central Park West, New York, NY 10024-5194-212-875-5400
New York Public Library, Grand Central Station, PO Box 4154, New York, NY 10163-4154
Smithsonian Institution, Washington, D.C. 20560
Strong Museum Library, 1 Manhattan Square Drive, Rochester, NY 14607-3941716-263-2700
Winterthur/Museum/Garden/Library, Winterthur, DE 19735

PICTURE CREDITS

Tools and materials, pages 14–17, and original cards, pages 10–13 (courtesy of the Laura Seddon Collection, Manchester Metropolitan University) © Sheila Sturrock
Fabrics, page 18, © www.flaxpr.com; Laura Ashley, www.LauraAshley.com
Buttons, page 18, © www.flickr.com; Briebeest
Sequins, page 19, © www.flickr.com;Erin!
Indian elephant, page 32, © Helen Lambert, www.earthskyart.com
Rose, page 34, © Dianne Robinson, www.versterre.com
Watercolour house, page 88, © Lyndsay Russel, www.driftwood-dreams.co.uk
Barn, page 98, Queen's View, page 118, © Tim Inglis

INDEX

To request a full catalogue of GMC titles, please contact:

GMC Publications,
Castle Place, 166 High Street, Lewes,
East Sussex, BN7 1XU, United Kingdom

Tel: 01273 488005
Fax: 01273 402866

www.thegmcgroup.com